POSTCARD HISTORY SERIES

Rockford

1900–WORLD WAR I

JImmy Ward in His Spectacular Flight Over the *Register-Gazette* Building, 1911.
In aviation's 1910s Exhibition Era, pioneering aviators like Jimmy Ward performed nationwide at thousands of locally-organized flight exhibitions, which were popular crowd-drawing events spearheaded by "Aero Clubs" and aviation-minded business organizations looking to advance the fledgling U.S. aviation industry. Rockford would prove no exception, hosting two of the nation's earliest aviation exhibitions in 1911 and 1912. Ward and famed fellow aviator Beckwith Havens visited Rockford from August 4th–6th, 1911 for a three-day Rockford & Interurban Railway Co. flying exhibition, part of local efforts to jump-start commercial aviation in Rockford. Here, Ward pilots his Curtiss Model D biplane, *Shooting Star*, over downtown's riverfront *Register-Gazette* Building. At such major, multi-day exhibitions, aviation enthusiasts were able to buy souvenir Real-Photo postcards depicting highlights from only a day or two before. (Courtesy: Mathew J. Spinello.)

POSTCARD HISTORY SERIES

Rockford

1900–WORLD WAR I

Eric A. Johnson

ARCADIA

Published by Arcadia Publishing,
an imprint of Tempus Publishing, Inc.
Charleston SC, Chicago, Portsmouth NH,
San Francisco

Printed in Great Britain.

Library of Congress Catalog Card Number: 2003105117

For all general information contact Arcadia Publishing at:
Telephone 843-853-2070
Fax 843-853-0044
E-Mail sales@arcadiapublishing.com
For customer service and orders:
Toll-Free 1-888-313-2665

Visit us on the internet at http://www.arcadiapublishing.com

This book is dedicated to my wife Barbara, daughter Evelyn, and son Andrew,
in grateful appreciation for their love and support.
This book is also dedicated in loving memory of my first born infant son,
Samuel Christopher Johnson.

(*Front Cover*) WEST STATE STREET. Looking east on West State toward Main Street in the heart of downtown Rockford's bustling "Loop" business district, the six-story Ashton's Dry Goods Building (1904–84), 301–05 West State, is seen at far left, followed by the Italianate-styled *c.* 1876 Samuel Stern Block, 211 West State, shown housing C.F. Henry Clothing Co. At far right is Rockford National Bank's seven-story Rockford Trust Building, 202–06 West State Street. While Ashton's is long a memory, the art deco-remodeled Stern Block and the now eleven-story Trust Building endure.

(*Back Cover*) CIVIL WAR VETERANS, SONS OF VETERANS AND SPANISH WAR VETERANS ON PARADE IN FRONT OF MEMORIAL HALL, DECORATION DAY, 1914. Established in the 1860s to decorate the graves of Civil War soldiers, Decoration Day quickly grew to encompass the poignant graveyard speeches and patriotic parades that mark today's Memorial Day. Given Decoration Day's still-strong Civil War roots in the early 1900s, Rockford's downtown Decoration Day parade drew thousands of spectators and hundreds of participants.

CONTENTS

Acknowledgments   6

Introduction   7

1.   Around the Town   9

2.   The Public Domain   33

3.   Rockford Business and Industry   45

4.   Residential Rockford   53

5.   Planes, Trains, and Automobiles   63

6.   College Town   69

7.   Three Cheers for Rockford High School   73

8.   A Legacy of Caring   77

9.   Camp Grant   95

10. A River Runs Through It   105

11. The Life and Times of Harlem Park   111

12. Parks and Recreation   119

13. Roosevelt in Rockford   127

ACKNOWLEDGMENTS

The decade-long creation of this book has been a far-from-solitary experience. I am deeply indebted to numerous individuals for their assistance in making this book a reality.

While the bulk of postcards included herein are drawn from my personal collection, I am extremely grateful to Rockford's Midway Village & Museum Center and avid Rockford postcard collectors Mary Lou Yankaitis, Mathew J. Spinello, and Mark D. Fry for graciously opening their collections to "fill in the gaps."

I am deeply indebted to Midway Village & Museum Center curator Rosalyn Robertson for coordinating the 228 high-quality CD-ROM scans included in this book.

I owe many thanks to John L. Molyneaux, curator of the Rockford Public Library's downtown Local History & Genealogy Room, for reading my manuscript and making several valuable suggestions and corrections. I'm also grateful for his multi-year assistance guiding me through the library's extensive local history archives as I researched images for this book.

Also, my deepest gratitude goes to the "above-and-beyond" assistance of the librarians overseeing the Rockford Public Library's downtown Reference Desk, particularly for their exceedingly gracious accommodation of my near-endless requests for the library's archival "Rockfordiana" collection of old newspaper clippings.

I also owe a great debt of gratitude to my friends-turned-family, Rockford residents Mike and Kay Douglas, for their warm and generous hospitality during my many research trips over the years. And a special thanks goes to Kay, an award-winning longtime English instructor at Rockford's Jefferson and West High Schools, for her professional input and suggestions regarding the evolving manuscript.

My thanks are also extended to Jerry Kortman and George "Doc" Slafkosky, co-owners of downtown Rockford's J.R. Kortman Center for Design. As ardent fellow Rockford historic preservationists and local history buffs, their longstanding enthusiasm for this book project has been a great source of inspiration.

I'm deeply grateful for the enthusiastic support of Jessica Belle Smith, Arcadia Publishing's Illinois acquisitions editor. A strong believer in my multi-volume Rockford postcard history series from the start, Jessica ably spearheaded the effort to make my longtime dream an ink-and-paper reality.

And last, but certainly not least, most of all I offer my heartfelt thanks to my family—wife Barbara, daughter Evelyn, and son Andrew—for their loving support and understanding during my long preoccupation with researching and writing this book.

Opposite: **GREAT ATLANTIC & PACIFIC TEA CO. (A&P) ROUTE SALES DELIVERY WAGON, 1908.** This colorful vermilion, black, and gold horse-drawn sales wagon would disappear with the 1917 advent of brick-and-mortar A&P supermarkets in Rockford. A&P once served thousands of smaller communities with its 5,000-wagon "stores on wheels" route sales division. A&P salesmen solicited orders door-to-door, bringing housewives a large array of goods, including coffee, tea, spices, baking power, condiments, household items, sugar, flour, cocoa, butter, and canned goods.

INTRODUCTION

"No man fit to be called a historian ever finished his work without feeling the inadequacy of his own powers, or of any conceivable human means, to reproduce the little fragment of history which he has chosen . . . "

—William Roscoe Thayer, *The Atlantic Monthly,* November 1918

The seeds for this book were planted quite innocently in 1987 when I acquired my first vintage postcard—a color 1910 view of West State Street in downtown Rockford—while prowling for bargains at a Labor Day antique show.

A longtime Rockford history buff, I was deeply struck by the postcard's nostalgic glimpse of West State Street in the heart of downtown's bustling "Loop" retail district. Fascinated with the postcard, it wasn't long before I purchased other Rockford postcards in what is a still-unsated collecting passion. Those early cards served as the foundation for a postcard collection now encompassing 500-plus views of Rockford and Loves Park spanning 1900–2003.

Vintage postcards provide a fascinating and unique avenue for observing Rockford's history and evolution with their visual record of the common Rockfordian's view of the important institutions of the city: home, school, church, work, and play. This assembly of vintage postcards displays a rich photographic record of the accomplishments of past generations of men and women who built and advanced Rockford from a small northern Illinois prairie outpost into a major industrial powerhouse city, known worldwide for the quality of its people and products.

Chicago's 1893 Columbian Exposition popularized the postcard in the United States. Shortly

after the turn-of-the-century, when postcards became a national rage, they arrived in Rockford and enjoyed several decades of widespread popularity. Thanks to this postcard craze, we're blessed with an outstanding visual record of Rockford's progress—the people, places, and events that shaped its history and evolution in the early 20th century.

In this book, I have not attempted to provide an exhaustive accounting of the city's history, but rather have endeavored to produce a complimentary volume to join several excellent histories produced in recent years, most notably Jon Lundin's 1989 *Rockford: An Illustrated History* and Rockford *Register Star* columnist Pat Cunningham's 2001 *Rockford: Big Town, Little City*.

In writing this book, my goal has been to produce a unique photographic essay of Rockford history from 1900 through World War I through the visual medium of picture postcards, discussing the relevance of the people, places, institutions, and events pictured. These postcards provide a fascinating and enlightening view of Rockford life in the early decades of the "American Century."

One needn't be a deltiologist (postcard collector) to appreciate and enjoy the assembled scenes of Rockford, given the fact that many area residents and expatriate Rockfordians alike have a deep abiding appreciation for the city's history and its wonderful buildings, businesses, and institutions, many of which endure to this day.

While many Rockford structures, particularly downtown, were razed in the 1950s, 1960s, 1970s, and early 1980s under the popular civic banners of "progress" and "urban renewal," many of the postcards included herein reveal that Rockford was luckily spared some of the wholesale destruction witnessed in America's other urban centers.

Over the years, the images in my ever-growing postcard collection have spurred me to learn more about the city's history. That passion for Rockford history eventually led to the creation of this book.

It is with great pleasure that I present this illustrated history of Rockford. It's my hope that these vintage postcards stir your interest in discovering Rockford's rich history.

WEST STATE STREET, WEST OF MAIN STREET, LOOKING EAST. The 1987 purchase of this postcard, my first vintage Rockford card, would eventually lead to the creation of this book. Visible at left center are Ashton's Dry Goods and the Italianate-styled *c.* 1876 Samuel Stern Block, shown housing C.F. Henry Clothing Co. At right (from left) is Rockford National Bank's Trust Building, John R. Porter Company's "Porter's Corner" drug store, John Beath's 45-room National Hotel in the *c.* 1872 Horsman Block, and the Hayes Dentist practice anchoring the Lewis Block. With the notable exceptions of the art deco-remodeled Stern Block and today's taller Trust Building, nearly all of the buildings pictured have been razed. Porter's and the Horsman and Lewis Blocks were demolished for the *c.* 1929 Pen-Met Building (1929-), part of today's Stewart Square.

One
AROUND THE TOWN

NELSON HOTEL, 306 SOUTH MAIN STREET, 1906. Rockford's leading hotel, the $250,000 Nelson (1892–1959) was built by Nelson Knitting Co. President William Nelson with the financial backing of his brothers, Fritz and Oscar. The 165-room hotel was named in honor of their father, John Nelson (1830–83), an 1852 immigrant Swede whose parallel-row knitting machine revolutionized the nation's textile industry and spawned Rockford's once-sizable knitting industry. Construction of a $400,000, seven-story annex added 200 guest rooms in 1919.

NELSON HOTEL LOBBY, 1915. With its elaborate Crystal Ballroom and magnificent skylighted lobby, the popular Nelson Hotel was one of Rockford's premiere gathering and lodging spots. As Rockford's showplace hotel, the Nelson hosted numerous notables including popular orator William Jennings Bryan, U.S. Presidents Theodore Roosevelt and William Howard Taft, famed World War I general John Joseph "Black Jack" Pershing, and federal-judge-turned-major-league-baseball-commissioner Kenesaw Mountain Landis.

HOTEL LELAND, 329 SOUTH MAIN STREET. Opened in 1911, the 67-room Hotel Leland (1911–90) operated under the Leland name until 1917, when it became the Hotel Edward. Known as Hotel Chandler after 1927, the hotel lived out its final decades as a low-income residence hotel. The Chandler and several adjacent South Main structures were purchased by the city for urban renewal and demolished in 1990, replaced by a municipal parking lot. (Courtesy: Midway Village & Museum Center.)

THE *ROCKFORD MORNING STAR* BUILDING, 127–29 NORTH WYMAN STREET, 1913. Built by grocery wholesaler Burr Brothers Co. in 1883, the Democratic *Rockford Morning Star* took occupancy of this building in 1908. Doomed by a widening of tiny Wyman Street, this building was razed and replaced in 1927 by the National Register-listed $300,000 art deco-styled *Morning Star* Building that currently anchors the site, long home to Rockford-based Pioneer Life and today housing Morrisey Law Offices. Following its merger with the competing *Register-Gazette* and *Daily Republic*, the *Morning Star* moved to the new riverfront Rockford News Tower in 1932.

MAIN STREET, LOOKING SOUTH, 1916. Orpheum Circuit's prestigious $39,980 Palace Theater, 115–17 North Main, anchored downtown's west side "Loop" business district from 1915–53. In its vaudeville heydays, the Palace offered seven-day-a-week vaudeville by such notables as magician Harry Houdini, singing cowboy Roy Rogers, singer Sammy Davis Jr., and popular headlining comedians including George Burns and Gracie Allen, Edgar Bergen, Jack Benny, and Bob Hope. Closed in 1953, the Palace housed dime store F.W. Woolworth Co. from 1956–83 and was demolished for downtown renewal in 1984.

MAIN STREET SOUTH OF STATE STREET. English immigrant Thomas Chick's 50-room Chick Hotel, 123 South Main, was a small but popular Rockford hostelry from 1883–1923. Sold to Milwaukeean John A. Saye in 1923, the renamed Elms Hotel continued in business until 1968. The enduring National Register-listed Chick Hotel Building, built in 1857 by Dr. R.P. Lane and Rockford bankers Thomas D. Robertson and Charles H. Spafford, was remodeled into a hotel in the 1870s, initially under the Edwards House and Griggs House names.

HEART OF BUSINESS DISTRICT, WEST STATE STREET LOOKING EAST. Seen at center is downtown Rockford's bustling streetcar "Transfer Corner" at West State and Wyman. The askew State Street Bridge has its roots in founder Germanicus Kent's 1836 refusal to allow Winnebago County surveyor Don Alonzo Spaulding to realign his west side street grid to match the street plat of Daniel Shaw Haight's east side settlement. Had Kent relented, the "awkward" State, Jefferson, and Chestnut–Walnut thoroughfare alignments on both sides of the Rock would today "harmonize as though there had been no river dividing the town."

INTERIOR OF ROCKFORD NATIONAL BANK, TRUST BUILDING, 1914. Founded in 1891 by land developer, mayor, and businessman Gilbert Woodruff, high-flying Rockford National Bank ranked as Rockford's largest bank until its Great Depression demise, an ironic ending for a bank that billed itself as "The Big Strong Bank" in 8-foot rooftop neon letters. The bank's South Main Street lobby, common by the day's standards, featured lavish marble, tile, onyx, and brass. Rockford Ice Hogs Professional Hockey, Inc., founded in 1999, today occupies much of the building's ground floor.

THE TRUST BUILDING, 202–06 WEST STATE STREET. Fast-growing Rockford National Bank and its Rockford Trust Co. division built this enduring seven-story "Chicago-style" structural steel and brick office building along West State between Main and Wyman in 1907. Already Rockford's tallest "skyscraper," an additional four stories were added in 1922. Rockford National Bank and Rockford Trust Co. anchored the Trust Building until their Great Depression closure in 1931.

North Side State Street Bridge, Rockford, Ill.

Chuck and me were in Chicago the last week with Strane.

water.

NORTH SIDE STATE STREET BRIDGE. Burr Brothers Wholesale Grocers' (1883–1936) *c.* 1909 warehouse at 216–22 North Water Street (left) and Fred G. Shoudy's *c.* 1910 Rockford Wholesale Grocery Co. warehouse, 118–30 North Water, remain familiar sights along downtown's east bank waterfront. In 1936, Rockford Wholesale (1887–1952) acquired Burr Brothers, consolidating operations at the Burr warehouse. It has since converted to marina and other commercial operations. In 1979–80, Rockford Century Group oversaw a $6 million renovation of the Rockford Wholesale building into its Waterside Building office development.

SOUTH MAIN STREET, LOOKING NORTH FROM CHESTNUT STREET. Along with State Street, Main Street was a popular downtown destination for shopping, banking, dining, entertainment, and lodging. Figuring prominently at left center is the European Plan-styled Illinois Hotel, a popular 70-room hostelry under the Illinois and Milner names from 1908 to 1965. Urban renewal in the 1970s saw the 200 block of South Main, pictured at left, transformed into the 10,000-seat Rockford MetroCentre civic auditorium and arena. (Courtesy: Midway Village & Museum Center.)

MAIN STREET, LOOKING SOUTH FROM WEST STATE STREET, 1912. The busy corner of West State and Main Streets was the heart of downtown's "Loop" commercial district. At left stands Rockford National Bank's prestigious Trust Building "skyscraper," followed by the high-rise Empire and William Brown buildings. At far right is the popular Porter's Corner pharmacy of John R. Porter Co. (1859–1965). Also anchoring the 100 block of South Main at right is A.W. Wheelock Crockery, department store D.J. Stewart & Co., and the Chick Hotel.

South Main St. looking North,
Rockford, Ill.

SOUTH MAIN STREET, LOOKING NORTH FROM ELM STREET. Pool halls like C.E. Osborne Billiards, 112 South Main, were a big Rockford business in the early 1900s, years when Rockford supported 28 competing billiard parlors—most along Seventh, State, and Main Streets. In those pool-playing heydays, Rockford hosted top players like Willie Mosconi, in addition to producing its own crop of local, state, regional, and national billiard champions. Seen at far right is George Ennenga's leading E&W Clothing House (1895–1965), 118–20 South Main.

15

ASHTON'S DRY GOODS, 301–05 WEST STATE STREET. Buoyed by his 1860–78 retailing success in Durand, English immigrant Andrew Ashton relocated to much-larger Rockford. A West State and Main "Loop" fixture from 1878 to 1974, Ashton's Dry Goods and its Rockford Dry Goods and Rockford Store successors occupied this $100,000 six-story "skyscraper" from 1904 to 1974. The largely vacant Ashton Building and two neighboring West State structures were demolished for a 300-car parking deck in 1984. (Courtesy: Midway Village & Museum Center.)

CHURCH STREET SOUTH FROM FOREST CITY NATIONAL BANK, 328–30 WEST STATE STREET. Forest City National Bank's distinctive Sumner Building (1890–2001) was named in honor of Pecatonica-born bank vice president E.B. Sumner, a prominent lawyer, city attorney, state legislator, and state senator. In 1923, Forest City relocated to its new high-rise headquarters at 401 West State, today's Enterprise Building. Later home to Bolender's Jewelers and Downtown Discount Drugs, the Sumner Building was razed for redevelopment in 2001. (Courtesy: Midway Village & Museum Center.)

WILLIAM BROWN BUILDING, 228–30 SOUTH MAIN STREET. Built in 1891–92 by People's State Bank, the $140,000 Romanesque Revival-styled William Brown Building was inspired by Chicago's famed Rookery Building. Named for English immigrant William Brown (1819–91), a prominent Rockford attorney, justice-of-the-peace, mayor, state legislator, and 20-year circuit court judge, the National Register-listed Brown Building has long been one of downtown's premier commercial properties. In 2000–01, Rockford developer William Charles Investments redeveloped the Brown's upper floors into 30 loft apartments.

GRAND OPERA HOUSE, 113–17 NORTH WYMAN STREET, 1908. Among the Midwest's largest theaters at 1500 seats, Rockford's Oriental-themed $25,000 Grand Opera House (1881–1917) hosted plays, concerts, musical performances, and lectures. Headliners included Shakespearean actor Edwin Booth, actress Ethel Barrymore, suffragist Susan B. Anthony, and author Oscar Wilde. Eclipsed by newer upstarts, the Opera House operated as a silent picture and burlesque house from 1915 to 1917 and was razed in 1926.

MEAD BUILDING, 301–05 SOUTH MAIN STREET, 1909. Built out of the fiery ruins of the original Mead store, the D.R. Mead & Co. Building (*c.* 1904) remains a familiar part of Rockford's downtown landscape. Founded in 1899 as purveyors of "furniture, carpets, crockery, stoves and undertaking," Mead gave way to A.E. Cutler Furniture Co. in 1917 and Hanley Furniture Co. in 1951. A furniture-retailing center from 1904 to 1993, the Mead Building more recently has housed the Fifth Precinct nightclub, the Rockford Brewing Co. brewpub, and Lots A Pasta Movie & Music Café.

EMPIRE BUILDING, 202–06 SOUTH MAIN STREET, 1910. Rising from the ashes of the *c.* 1856 Hotel Holland, Rockford department store titan Duncan James (D.J.) Stewart bankrolled the 1900 construction of the highrise Empire Building. Designed by prolific Rockford architect David S. Schureman, the Empire Building served as Tebala Shrine Temple until 1916 and D.J. Stewart & Co. headquarters until 1936. Condemned by the city in 1972, the Empire Building was demolished for a municipal parking lot in 1978.

NORTH MAIN STREET, 1910. Looking northeast toward Main and Mulberry from the roof of Ashton's Dry Goods, at right is the C.F. Henry Block (1896–1983), 119–21 North Main. At center is the $60,000 Church of the Christian Union (1888–1940). Organized in 1870 to promote liberal, non-denominational religious thought by 104 disenchanted members of First Baptist Church (*c.* 1858) and their ousted immigrant Scottish minister, Dr. Thomas Kerr, Church of the Christian Union relocated to 2101 Auburn Street in 1942 and to a $400,000 facility at 4845 Turner Street in 1966. Affiliated with the American Unitarian Association beginning in 1928, the congregation today operates as Unitarian Universalist Church.

WEST STATE STREET, 1912. Looking east on West State from the Colonial Theater (1910–24) and Ashton's Dry Goods, patriotism dominates Rockford's downtown landscape. In the late 1800s and early 1900s, patriotic parades and flag displays were common Decoration Day and Fourth of July traditions. Local patriotic fervor, fueled by Rockford's sizeable Civil War and Spanish-American War veterans community, only intensified with World War I and the establishment of Rockford's "Camp Grant" Army training cantonment. (Courtesy: Mark D. Fry.)

MENDELSSOHN HALL, 513–15 WEST STATE STREET. This distinctive building was constructed in 1899 by George Briggs and dubbed Mendelssohn Hall as a memorial to his wife, an avid member of Rockford's long-lived Mendelssohn Club (*c.* 1884), the nation's oldest continuously operating music club. The growing Mendelssohn Club met in second floor quarters until moving to North Main Street's newly built Chick Block in 1909. Razed in the mid-1980s for downtown renewal, the Mendelssohn Hall site now houses the Rockford Mass Transit District's downtown passenger terminal.

INTERIOR OF ADAM H. BOLENDER JEWELRY STORE, 313 WEST STATE STREET, 1909. Founded in 1896 by Adam H. Bolender, Bolender's Jewelers was a longtime downtown retailing fixture. Selling watches, diamonds, jewelry, clocks, silverware, and optical goods, Bolender's relocated to its longtime home in downtown's recently-razed Sumner Building at South Church and West State in the 1920s. Mirroring the 1960s–1980s retail exodus from downtown Rockford, Bolender's relocated to the Brynwood Square shopping center, 2589 North Mulford Road.

TEMPERANCE PARADE. Looking west from the marquee of the Palm (State) Theater, 105 West State Street, a temperance parade passes through the 100 and 200 blocks of West State Street. From 1865 to 1933, Rockford was a famed temperance town, home to one of the nation's charter Women's Christian Temperance Union (*c.* 1874) chapters. But local teetotaling sensibilities were far from unanimous. The city regularly vacillated between "wet" and "dry," depending on who was in city hall. (Courtesy: Midway Village & Museum Center.)

We invite you to call and learn more about our
"Haddorff Pianos", and see our extensive line of sheet music.
O. J. WIGELL
"The Oldest music house in Rockford."
107 W. State St.,   Rockford, Ill.

O.J. WIGELL PIANO STORE, 107 WEST STATE STREET. Leading music dealer Oscar J. Wigell was an early prominent downtown "Loop" retailing anchor. The "oldest music house in Rockford," Wigell's specialized in Rockford-made Haddorff pianos, small instruments, and an "extensive line of sheet music." Organized by famed Rockford industrialist, philanthropist, and venture capitalist P.A. Peterson, (C.A.) Haddorff Piano Co. (1901–53) was a leading firm in Rockford's once-dominant furniture industry and ranked as one of the world's largest premier piano makers. (Courtesy: Mark D. Fry.)

AMERICAN INSURANCE CO., 304–06 NORTH MAIN STREET. Founded during the Civil War, Rockford Insurance Co. was acquired by Newark-based American Insurance Co. in 1899. In 1904, American built this $100,000 brick and terra cotta "Western Department" headquarters, a structure "built for a thousand years." Home to Rockford-based PioneerLife since 1939, the building was vacated in 2002 and awaits reuse following Indiana-based Conseco's massive downsizing of its once-extensive downtown Rockford Pioneer operations, acquired for $480 million in 1997.

ROCKFORD GAS, LIGHT AND COKE CO., 201 MULBERRY STREET, 1907. Established in 1855, Rockford Gas, Light and Coke built this headquarters in 1857. Ground floor showrooms displayed the latest in gas and electric appliances, lighting fixtures, and heating equipment. Vacated in 1931 for the new Gas & Electric Building, this building subsequently housed Rockford Savings & Loan until 1959. Neighboring Central National Bank razed the "Gas Light" and adjacent Florence May Apartments (right) in 1959–62 for expanded parking and drive-up banking facilities. The sites are now a municipal parking lot.

COLISEUM, 913–23 WEST STATE STREET, 1912. Contractor Standish Budlong's pre-World War I Coliseum served as a skating rink, dance hall, and community assembly hall until it was eclipsed in popularity by the new Inglaterra ballroom and the Tebala Shrine's much-larger auditorium. The largely idled Coliseum, briefly operated as a theater from 1919 to 1920, was sold in 1921 to the Catholic Diocese of Rockford for use by St. Thomas High School. Remodeled into five classrooms and a multi-purpose assembly hall, the Coliseum was later converted into a gymnasium. The Coliseum was razed following the 1962 closure of St. Thomas.

ROCKFORD BUILDING, 516–30 WEST STATE STREET, 1911. A longtime anchor of the southeast corner of West State and Winnebago, the Rockford Building housed the 50-room Hotel Blackhawk. The Rockford Building was demolished in 1927 for the enduring terra cotta and granite art deco-styled Blackhawk Building. Home to Rockford Life from 1956 to 1986, the remodeled four-story Blackhawk Building has housed the Janet Wattles Center public health clinic since 1988.

ORPHEUM THEATER, 118 NORTH MAIN STREET, 1913. Founded as a nickelodeon in 1901 in a converted 1860s livery stable, Rockford's Orpheum Theater was transformed into a popular vaudeville house in 1906 under the new ownership of A.J. Shimp, who had opened East State Street's Bijou in 1904 as Rockford's first dedicated vaudeville venue. Extensively remodeled in 1908, the Orpheum by 1915 was eclipsed in grandeur by then-parent Orpheum Circuit's new Palace Theater, 117 North Main. Following the Palace's debut, the Orpheum operated exclusively as a movie house until 1937, when it was replaced by the Art Moderne-styled Times Theater (1938–83), 226 North Main.

INTERIOR OF ORPHEUM THEATER FROM THE STAGE, 1912. As "The House That Never Fails to Please," A.J. Shimp's Orpheum Theater reigned as Rockford's premiere early vaudeville and "photo-play" palace. During its 1906–15 vaudeville years, the Orpheum hosted numerous stars including early silent film comedian Ben Turpin (1874–1940) and heavyweight boxing champion John L. Sullivan (1858–1918), widely regarded as "the last of the great bare-knuckle fighters." The 900-seat Orpheum, seen here as experienced by its vaudeville headliners, offered main floor, balcony, loge, and parquet seating. (Courtesy: Mark D. Fry.)

MAJESTIC THEATER AND ARMORY BLOCK, 113–25 NORTH CHURCH STREET, 1911. Prominent attorney B.A. Knight's $25,000 Armory Block (left) was home to Rockford High School basketball games and Rockford's World War I-era Companies H&K. Extensively remodeled, the Armory Block housed retailer Sears from 1928 to 1956 and was later demolished for parking. A nickelodeon turned "high-class" 10¢ vaudeville house and movie theater, the Majestic Theater (1909–12) was converted to other uses and later razed for real estate developer Max Liebling's 1951 Nu-State Building, 119 North Church.

EAST SIDE INN, 104 NORTH MADISON STREET, 1914. Built in 1889 by the Rockford YMCA and renovated into the Merlein Block office building in 1906, this National Register-listed Richardsonian Romanesque structure operated as the 60-room East Side Inn from 1909 to 1968. Demolition seemed imminent for the deteriorating structure in 1985. Spared the wrecker's ball when it was named an East Rockford Historic District landmark, the building was sold and underwent a $1.6 million restoration into today's East Side Centre office building.

LOBBY, EAST SIDE INN. This postcard offers a rare view of the East Side Inn's cozy lobby in the hotel's early heydays under the 1909–17 ownership of prominent grocery wholesaler and retailer Fred L. Burr. The 60-room East Side Inn was one of only a handful of east side hostelries. With Rockford's Illinois Central, Milwaukee Road, Burlington Route and Chicago & Northwestern depots located on South Main Street, most of Rockford's leading and largest hotels were concentrated on downtown's west side.

MARKET DAY AT CITY MARKET, 713 EAST STATE STREET, 1915. Today a weekend summer novelty, this was downtown's Shumway farmer's market in its 1910s heydays. In 1904, pioneer Rockford seed man Roland H. Shumway (1842–1925) donated this site to the city with the proviso that it preserve the public farmer's market in perpetuity "for the benefit of all and the poor especially." This large Shumway Market crowd was a typical year-round scene on Tuesdays, Thursdays, and Saturdays. (Courtesy: Midway Village and Museum Center.)

R.H. SHUMWAY MARKET PLACE "COMFORT STATION," 713 EAST STATE STREET.
Following Roland Shumway's 1904 creation and donation of his public farmer's market, the city erected this "suitable stone entrance archway" in 1905 as part of its acceptance of Shumway's gift. Offering public bathroom facilities for market vendors and patrons, the "comfort station" was razed in 1920 to make way for architect Charles Bradley's current Shumway Market building. (Courtesy: Midway Village & Museum Center.)

INTERIOR OF KEELING'S DRUG STORE, 402 EAST STATE STREET. The opulence of Keeling's Drug Store stands in stark contrast to the spartan, cookie-cutter pharmacies of today. Expatriate Yankee pharmacist brothers James H. and W.B. Keeling came to Rockford from Brooklyn in 1861, selling pharmaceuticals, cigars, and Hudnut-branded perfumes and toilet articles until their 1911 retirement. In recent decades, the old Keeling Drug Store housed Zant Office Equipment and Supplies. (Courtesy: Midway Village & Museum Center.)

27

EAST STATE STREET, LOOKING WEST TOWARD FIRST STREET, 1912. Though overshadowed in importance and prominence by Rockford's prestigious west side "Loop" downtown, which was centered around West State and Main Streets, the east side downtown that developed along East State Street nevertheless enjoyed its own vibrancy. Major buildings at left include the George M. Blake Block, 403–05 East State, the *c.* 1884 Third National Bank Building, 401 East State, and the Manufacturers National Bank Building, 327–27 East State. Pictured at far left is the Robert E. Doxsee & Son shoe store, 407 East State.

EAST STATE STREET, LOOKING EAST FROM SECOND STREET. Demolition and fires took their toll on Rockford's downtown landscape. Built in 1883 at 502–06 East State, the I.E. Cutter Block (left) was destroyed in a spectacular 1968 arson fire. The enduring Queen Anne–styled John H. Hutchins Block (center), 508–14 East State, was built in three stages between 1880 and 1900. The mammoth P.A. Peterson Building (1911–73), 516–28 East State, housed the popular Hess Brothers department store. Visible above the Peterson Building is the steeple of State Street Baptist Church, built in 1868 and destroyed in a massive 1949 fire.

HESS BROTHERS & CO. "BIG STORE," P.A. PETERSON BUILDING, 516–28 EAST STATE STREET. Billed as "Rockford's Mammoth New Department Store" at its 1911 debut, Carl and Milton Hess' downtown Hess Brothers store lived up to its hype with its 19,000-square-foot store in the newly-built P.A. Peterson Building. Sold to Peoria-based Block & Kuhl in 1928 and Chicago's Carson Pirie Scott & Co. in 1959, the East State retailing anchor closed in 1963. The long-vacant Peterson Building was razed in 1973. (Courtesy: Mark D. Fry.)

SEVENTH STREET NORTH FROM FIFTH AVENUE. A massive influx of Swedish immigrants riding the Galena & Chicago Union Railroad west from Chicago to end-of-the-line Rockford in 1852 paved the way for the development of a new downtown as newly-arrived immigrant Swedes developed their Sjunde Gatan (Seventh Street) in an 11-block area south of East State Street on the city's near southeast side. The immigrant ethnic enclave included Swedish-language churches, Swedish-American owned stores, and ethnic Swede cultural associations and organizations.

THE DAYLIGHT STORE (EKEBERG'S DRY GOODS), 427–29 SEVENTH STREET. Brothers Gust, Albert, and Joseph Ekeberg joined forces in 1908 to found Ekeberg's Dry Goods in the window-laden Daylight Store Lundberg Building. The since-razed building also housed the Hotel Kent, one of several small hotels serving passengers arriving at Seventh Street's small Chicago & Northwestern depot. Ekeberg's, which moved to the nearby Reliance Building in 1923, returned to this site in 1928, operating here until its 1958 demise. At its height, Ekeberg's also operated a second location at 1019 Broadway. (Courtesy: Midway Village & Museum Center.)

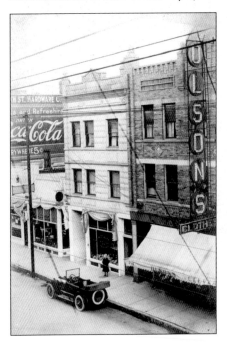

200 BLOCK OF SEVENTH STREET. While the businesses have changed, these Seventh Street buildings remain a familiar sight today. At left with the Coca-Cola sign is the Seventh Street Hardware Co. Building, 208 Seventh. The low-rise Cheshire Building at center, built in 1911 at 212 Seventh, has housed Rockford Mattress Co. since 1928. At far right is the Palm Building, 218–20 Seventh, built in 1909 by 1874 Swedish immigrant J.A. Palm, a prominent local contractor said to have "built the larger part of the big stores on Seventh Street." (Courtesy: Midway Village & Museum Center.)

SVEA MUSIC HALL, 326–30 SEVENTH STREET. In the late 19th and early 20th century, choral singing was all the rage in Rockford. Founded in 1890 by Alfred G. Larson and S.H.E. Oberg, the ethnic Swedish Svea Soner Singing Society counted famed Rockford industrialists Levin Faust and Pehr August "P.A." Peterson among its members. Built in 1892–93 and named for its longtime anchor, $54,000 Svea Music Hall was designed by prolific Rockford architect David S. Shureman. The National Register-listed structure was destroyed in a 1980 blaze.

PEOPLE'S PHARMACY, 402 SEVENTH STREET. As seen at right, lavishly-appointed marble soda fountain lunch counters were once a popular staple of drug stores like Amel E. Freburg's People's Pharmacy. Now vacant and awaiting reuse, this enduring and distinctive building has housed a number of businesses including People's Pharmacy, successor Rudelius Drugs, art dealer Rockford Gallery, the Seventh Street Recreation Luncheonette restaurant, and, most recently, nail salon P.T. Nails. (Courtesy: Mark D. Fry.)

14TH AVENUE (BROADWAY) EAST FROM SEVENTH STREET, 1911. Today's Broadway retail business district was just beginning to come of age, as evidenced by these impressive brick and masonry buildings built just a few years prior along once-rural 14th Avenue. An enduringly familiar sight is the *c.* 1905 Tureson Block (far right), 1101–03 Broadway. A distant memory is the adjacent Hultberg Block, 1105–07 Broadway. (Courtesy: Mary Lou Yankaitis.)

SOUTH MAIN STREET, LOOKING NORTH FROM MORGAN STREET. The longtime home of Rockford's immigrant Italian community and the early 1913–20 home of its small Jewish enclave, this near southwest side "South Rockford" retailing district was a popular shopping, dining and entertainment destination, particularly with Rockford's Italian-American community. Fondly remembered South Main anchors include the Capitol and Rialto theaters and Julius & Mayme Miller's Fair Store department store. Today, South Main is revitalizing as an ethnic Hispanic retail area. Anchoring South Main and Morgan at right is the enduring *c.* 1898 W.F. Hudler Building, 1030–32 South Main.

Two
THE PUBLIC DOMAIN

U.S. POST OFFICE AND FEDERAL BUILDING, 401 SOUTH MAIN STREET, 1909. This Romanesque red sandstone building served as Rockford's first federally built main post office and federal courthouse. Built on the southwest corner of South Main and Green Streets, this structure was dedicated on October 1, 1885, and served the city until it was razed in 1932 to make way for a new main post office and federal building development on the same site.

ROCKFORD FIRE DEPARTMENT AERIAL LADDER TRUCK, 1911. The Rockford Fire Department's horse-drawn era began to draw to a close with the 1911 addition of several motorized firefighting units, including this $8,700 Seagraves "motor aerial hook and ladder truck" showcased outside Rockford City Hall. Assigned to Station No. 1, the truck boasted an air-cooled engine and spring-loaded 75-foot wooden extension ladder. Pictured from left to right are Arthur Wakeford, Capt. Thomas Blake, Lt. Charles Strom, Gust Hagman, Thomas Burbank, Harry Hudler, Phil Stromberg, and Charles Rockwood.

FIRE MARSHAL F.E. THOMAS, 1908. Rockford Fire Department Fire Marshal Frank E. Thomas poses outside Station 1, 212 South Church Street. A longtime department veteran, Thomas served for over 35 years from 1886 to 1921, including 20 years as fire chief from 1901 to 1921. Thomas presided over the 1911–18 transition from a horse-drawn department to a motorized firefighting force. Thomas was succeeded by Stephan T. Julian (1921–22) and Thomas D. Blake (1922–46). (Courtesy: Midway Village & Museum Center.)

ENGINE COMPANY NO. 1, 212 SOUTH CHURCH STREET, 1908. Founded as a volunteer force in 1855, the Rockford Fire Department became a paid force in 1881. To mark the 27th anniversary of the paid department, the Rockford Fire Department issued a series of seven postcards. Shown outside Station No. 1 (1883–1958) are, from left to right, Thomas Burbank, Dan Malone, Charles Rockwood, Arthur Wakefield, Asst. Fire Chief Stephan T. Julian, Harry Agar, and Capt. John Cregan. (Courtesy: Midway Village & Museum Center.)

ENGINE COMPANY NO. 2, 414 WALNUT STREET, 1908. Shown outside Station No. 2 (1885–1926) are, from left to right, Captain Burt Randell, Frank Conrad, Uno Larson, A. Lander, Robert Ferguson, and Oscar Risberg. Nicknamed "Big Red," Station 2 was originally located on the northeast corner of South First and Walnut Streets, the site of today's "Old City Hall." With plans laid for city hall's construction in 1902, Station 2 was moved just east of its original site.

ENGINE COMPANY NO. 3, 1015 SOUTH MAIN STREET, 1908. Pictured outside Station No. 3 (1887–1955) are, from left to right, Captain Thomas Blake, R. Fitzgerald, E. Hamlin, E.T. Anderson, R. Stinstrom, and James Sullivan. Cost associated with developing Station 3 included $17,900 for the building, $368 for land, and $1,072 for furnishings. (Courtesy: Midway Village & Museum Center.)

ENGINE COMPANY NO. 4, 1115 SIXTH AVENUE, 1908. Staffing Engine Company No. 4 are, from left to right: Capt. Axel Hultin, John P. Larsen, E. Strand, H. Johnson, Andrew Bergstrom, Oscar Cruso, and H. Westberg. Engine Company No. 4, organized in 1886, and Hook and Ladder Company No. 2, formed in 1923, called this $4,472 c. 1893 fire station home until 1978. The Golden Agers Senior Center has occupied the old firehouse since 1981. (Courtesy: Mathew J. Spinello.)

ENGINE COMPANY NO. 5, 1528 18TH AVENUE, 1908. Organized in May 1902, Engine Company No. 5 was located at 1303 14th Avenue before relocating to this $8,352 firehouse in October 1907. Pictured outside Station 5 are, from left to right, Capt. Ernest Pearson, Oscar Johnson, and A. Hambloom. Currently vacant, the former firehouse has seen both residential and commercial use since its 1990 deactivation.

ENGINE COMPANY NO. 6, 1634 ELM STREET, 1908. Engine Company No. 6 was commissioned into service in 1907. This $7,752 facility served Rockford's west end until a new Station 6 facility opened in 1974 at 3329 West State Street. Shown here outside Engine Company 6 are, from left to right: Capt. William Julian, Matt Long, William Brennan, P. Kelley, O. Swenson, W.J. Malone, and Charles Chandler. Later home to St. Matthew Lodge, Station 6 was later razed. Today, the site is home to the Rockford Public School's expansive Ellis Arts Academy campus.

WATER WORKS, 100 PARK AVENUE. Rockford's riverfront Water Works headquarters and pumping/reservoir complex were located on the site of an ancient artesian well. Built in 1875, the Water Works complex met a fiery end in a spectacular 1953 extra-alarm arson fire. Following the blaze, the buildings were razed and the Water Works headquarters was relocated to 1111 Cedar Street. The riverfront site, long a municipal parking lot called the Water Works Lot, was redeveloped in the 1990s with the construction of a low-rise professional office building for law firm Hinshaw & Culbertson.

ROCKFORD, Ill. PUBLIC LIBRARY. MEMORIAL HALL.   Penfield's Book Store.

Since writing the previous card, I have rec'd a "Ceylon Bldg.

PUBLIC LIBRARY, 215 NORTH WYMAN STREET, 1904. Founded in 1872 as the second taxpayer-supported library in Illinois, fast-growing Rockford Public Library quickly outgrew its various rented downtown quarters. A fundraising drive to build a public library facility found a generous benefactor in Scottish-American steel magnate and philanthropist Andrew Carnegie (1835–1919), donor of Rockford's $80,000 Carnegie Library, built in 1902–03. Seeking to create the "library of the future," library director Jack Chitwood oversaw the 1962–65 construction of a three-story addition and the 1966–69 expansion and complete interior and exterior remodeling of the Carnegie Library, today hidden behind a veneering of Indiana limestone.

MEMORIAL HALL, 211 NORTH MAIN STREET. Built as Winnebago County's tribute to its Civil War and Spanish-American War casualties, $59,136 Memorial Hall was the first such structure of its kind built in the nation, dedicated in June 1903 by President Theodore Roosevelt in front of a crowd of 20,000. Memorial Hall has dodged the demolition bullet twice—in the 1960s and again in the mid-1980s. Designated an Illinois historic landmark in 1974 and listed on the prestigious National Register in 1976, Memorial Hall received a $1.5 million restoration in 1988–92.

ROCKFORD CITY HALL, 130 SOUTH FIRST STREET, 1911. Architect David S. Shureman's $100,000 red sandstone structure served as Rockford's first city hall from 1907 to 1941, when city hall relocated to the vacant nearby Manufacturer's National Bank Building. Thereafter, "Old City Hall" served as the Rockford Police Department headquarters until 1977. In 1994–95, Chicago developer Hank Zuba undertook a $2.5 million restoration of long-idled Old City Hall into a 31-unit apartment complex.

POLICE PATROL BARN, 1909. Rockford's Police Patrol Barn would soon pass into history with the addition of the Rockford Police Department's first motorized ambulance in 1913 and first motorized patrol cars and paddy wagons in 1914. Pictured (from left) are Homer Read and Luther Robinson in the Patrol Wagon, Fred Glenny at the helm of the *c.* 1883 Paddy Wagon, and Frank Burbank and James Chandler on horseback.

THE FOUNTAIN, COURTHOUSE SQUARE. The Grand Army of the Republic Auxiliary, an association of mothers, spouses, and widows of Civil War veterans, dedicated this zinc statue and fountain in tribute to Winnebago County's Civil War veterans in 1902. Located outside the West State Street Courthouse Square entrance to the 1878 Winnebago County Courthouse, the statue was later placed in a glass case inside the new 1969 courthouse. In 1985, this veteran's memorial was relocated to newly-created Statue Park outside Greenwood Cemetery, on the northeast corner of North Main and Auburn Streets in Rockford's North End Commons retail district.

Rockford, Ill., Court House

WINNEBAGO COUNTY COURTHOUSE. Envious of the new Stephenson County Courthouse in Freeport and finding Winnebago County government needed more room to grow as county seat Rockford transformed into a major industrial city, county supervisors laid plans to replace their *c.* 1844 Greek Revival/Grecian Doric wood frame courthouse with a larger, more pretentious facility.

Designed by Chicago architect Henry L. Gay in an architecturally eclectic French-Venetian-American style, Winnebago County's new $211,000 limestone-clad courthouse was built between 1876 and 1878. Construction was temporarily halted by a horrific May 11, 1877 structural collapse that left 7 dead and 14 injured.

Champaign architect J.W. Royer's enduring $326,000 annex, 403 Elm Street, was added in 1916–1918 to accommodate the growing county's needs. The adjoining $160,000 Youth Welfare Building, 401 Elm, was added in 1957.

Deteriorating, outgrown, and increasingly-outdated, the 1878 courthouse was demolished in 1969–70 following the completion of Winnebago County's new 10-story courthouse "tower," 400 West State Street.

NELSON BRIDGE, 15TH AVENUE. Rockford's first bridge spanning the Rock River at 15th Avenue/Marchesano Drive was built in 1892 at a cost of $17,075, a sum privately financed by Rockford textile titan William Nelson. The span lasted until 1934, when a $150,000 concrete Works Project Administration (WPA) bridge replaced it. The 15th Avenue WPA bridge was replaced with a new $2.9 million span in 1979–81.

Morgan St. Bridge, (Nearly 1000 feet in length), Rockford, Ill.

MORGAN STREET BRIDGE. The first bridge spanning the Rock River at Morgan Street was constructed in 1890. The Morgan Street Bridge, as pictured here, was reconstructed in 1917 and doubled in length to almost 1,000 feet. Upon its completion, the bridge was tested for soundness by running a 20-ton steamroller over the span.

3677. Chestnut Street Bridge, looking West, Rockford, Ill.

CHESTNUT STREET BRIDGE, LOOKING WEST. The City of Rockford recycled on a grand scale in 1890 when this *c.* 1872 steel trestle bridge was floated down river from State Street to serve as the city's first bridge at Chestnut Street. This structure served as the Chestnut Street Bridge until it was replaced with a steel and concrete span in 1917.

"NORTH END" OR "HIGH" BRIDGE, 1908. Connecting Auburn Street with Spring Creek Road, this $50,000 "North End" or "High" Bridge was built by Winnebago County in 1900–01. The bridge's most distinctive and aggravating feature was the 7.4 degree grade used to raise the bridge 25 feet over the Rock River to allow the excursion steamer *Illinois* to pass underneath, a feat still only accomplished by having the ship's smokestacks hinged so they could be lowered to pass under the bridge. New, lower bridges replaced this span in 1937 and 1987.

West State St. Rockford, Ill.

STATE STREET "GIRDER BRIDGE" WEST VIEW, 1906. A downtown fixture from 1891 to 1949, the city's $57,236 State Street "Girder Bridge" was built "wide enough to permit the speeding nag to pass its slow predecessor and strong enough to allow horses to go at full speed and electric [street] cars to spin along on scheduled time." Looking west toward West State's downtown "Loop" retailing district, pictured along the riverfront is the Women's Christian Temperance Union Temperance Headquarters (left) and the *Register-Gazette* Building housing the daily newspaper and Rockford Business College (right).

STATE STREET "GIRDER BRIDGE" EAST VIEW, 1910. Looking east toward East State Street from the WCTU Temperance Headquarters, one sees the *c.* 1891 State Street "Girder Bridge" as well as a number of east side downtown anchors including Rockford Lumber & Fuel Co., the Republican-leaning *Rockford Daily Republic* newspaper, and, in the distance at center, the enduring National Register-listed East Side Centre Building, once home to the Rockford YMCA and the East Side Inn.

Three
BUSINESS AND
INDUSTRY

WATER POWER DISTRICT SHOWING EDISON STATION, ROCKFORD ELECTRIC COMPANY.
Perhaps the most pivotal development in Rockford history was the 1851 development of the
Rockford Water Power Co. (1851–1963) and its enduring Rock River Fordam Dam. Erected
just south of downtown, the Fordam Dam harnessed Rock River waterpower—and later,
hydroelectric power—to energize the city's embryonic manufacturing base. Thanks to the Water
Power District dam, a long period of phenomenal industrial expansion ensued, helping Rockford
prosper into Illinois's "Second City" and one of the nation's premier manufacturing centers. The
current Fordam Dam, built 1904–10, is today used to adjust the Rock River's water level north
of the dam for recreational boating and flood control. (Courtesy: Mark D. Fry.)

BURSON KNITTING CO., 506 SOUTH MAIN STREET. A former Nelson Knitting Co. partner, William Worth Burson established rival Burson Knitting Co. in 1892, aided by Rockford industrialists Ralph Emerson, W.H. Ziock, and William E. Hinchliff. Specializing in the manufacture of Burson Fashioned Hose, women's cotton stockings, Burson opened this enduring 130,000-square-foot factory in 1915. Producing some 1,500 tons of product annually, the company ranked as Rockford's largest textile operation with 500 employees and nearly 2,000 knitting machines. Sold to Boston-based Kendall Co. in 1948, Burson's Rockford operations closed in a 1959 consolidation with Kendall's South Carolina operations.

HESS & HOPKINS LEATHER CO., 1101 ACORN STREET. Rockford once boasted the world's largest tannery in Hess & Hopkins (1866–1960), founded by Freeport Civil War veteran Luther M. Hess. Joined in 1877 by Rockford bookkeeper and farmer Theodore Hopkins, Hess by 1900 had grown the firm into a 6-acre, 200,000-square-foot tannery complex specializing in the manufacture of saddles, harnesses, horse collars, and other leather goods. At its peak, the firm employed 450 and tanned over 360 steer and cow hides daily. Mechanized farming and the automobile slowly but inexorably eroded demand for the company's leather products. The company liquidated following the 1960 death of Arthur T. Hopkins, the last direct descendant of the Hess and Hopkins families. The tannery was razed in 1968–69 for the Rockford Housing Authority's 210-unit Fairgrounds Valley housing project.

"I Use Greenlee Tools." Unlike most of Rockford's high-profile old-line manufacturing firms, Greenlee Brothers Co. wasn't native to Rockford. Identical twins Ralph S. and Robert L. Greenlee founded the firm in Chicago in 1862, producing a variety of woodworking tools that brought the brothers fame at the 1876 Philadelphia Exposition. Beset by labor woes and an outdated, inefficient, and landlocked facility, Greenlee moved to Rockford in 1904, selecting a site at 2136–40 12th Street in the Illinois Central's southeast side industrial rail loop. Expanded into metalworking tools in 1915, Rockford-based Greenlee was purchased in 1969 by Ex-Cell-O Corp. and by Rhode Island-based global industrial conglomerate Textron in 1986. Today, manufacturing tools for residential, commercial, and industrial wire and cable installation and maintenance, Greenlee relocated its Rockford headquarters and manufacturing operations to new state-of-the-art facilities near Greater Rockford Airport between 1982 and 1988.

W.F. AND JOHN BARNES CO., 301–11 SOUTH WATER STREET, 1913. Expatriate New York brothers William Fletcher, B. Frank, and John Barnes joined forces in 1872 to create Rockford's W.F. & John Barnes Co., a manufacturer of drills and lathes for iron- and wood-working. This sprawling riverfront factory (1889–1967) was designed by prominent Rockford architect William R. Keyt. Barnes would spawn three offshoots: (B. Frank) Barnes Drill Co. in 1907, John S. Barnes Co. in 1929, and Metal Cutting Tools Inc. in 1941. Later specializing in the manufacture of cutting and machine tools, Barnes was sold to New York-based Babcock & Wilcox Co. in 1963 and Michigan's Acme Precision Products, Inc. in 1982. Barnes' 500-employee Rockford operations were closed in a 1983 consolidation with Acme's Rochester, Michigan operations.

BARBER-COLMAN CO., 1300 ROCK STREET. Eighteen-year-old Howard Colman parlayed a $100 1891 loan from Wisconsin lumberman W.A. Barber into a 1904 patent and, eventually, an enduring global firm that today ranks as one of metro Rockford's larger employers. From its early focus on manufacturing textile machinery, Barber-Colman later broadened its scope into machine tools, temperature controls, and plastic molding. Barber-Colman's near southwest side Water Power District manufacturing complex, seen here, grew to encompass 15 buildings spanning 26 acres. The firm added its enduring Clifton Avenue manufacturing complex in Loves Park in 1953. The company's Rockford textile machinery business, seen here, was spun-off as Reed-Chatwood, Inc. (1984–99). One of the nation's largest privately-held companies by the mid-1980s, Barber-Colman was sold to Windsor, England-based Siebe plc in 1987 and London-based Invensys in 1999. Invensys sold Barber-Colman Aerospace to London's Smith's Industries in December 1999. (Courtesy: Mathew J. Spinello.)

ROCKFORD SUGAR REFINING CO. A short-lived city industry, beet sugar refining and Rockford were never synonymous like the city's more historically prominent industries—agricultural implements, furniture, textiles, machine tools, and fasteners. Established in 1896, Rockford Sugar Refining's Seminary Street factory transformed incoming railcars of raw sugar beets into sugar and molasses. Purchased in 1898 by Chicago-based Glucose Sugar Refining Co. and subsequently renamed, Glucose would close its Rockford refinery in 1906.

Skandia Furniture Co., Rockford, Ill.

SKANDIA FURNITURE CO., 1202 NORTH SECOND STREET. Rockford's predominantly Swedish furniture industry rivaled textiles and agricultural equipment for prominence in the late 1800s and early 1900s, employing thousands of local residents in furniture manufacturing and complementary supply industries. Skandia Furniture (1888–1941) once ranked as Rockford's largest furniture manufacturer, producing a variety of products including hall trees, "Viking" bookcases, cylinder desks, secretaries, and pillar extension pages in this two-block-long riverfront plant, built in 1890 as "the largest single building in the city devoted to the manufacture of furniture..." Fine examples of Skandia furniture can be viewed at Rockford's Erlander Home Museum.

FOREST CITY KNITTING CO. In the late 1800s and early 1900s, seven major knitting firms built Rockford into the nation's largest hosiery producer. Founded in 1890 by Rockford textile scions Fritz, William, and Oscar Nelson to produce cotton work socks, and later, cotton athletic socks, Forest City Knitting Co. occupied this picturesque 40,000-square-foot southeast side plant at Catherine and Magnolia Streets from 1890 until 1954, when Rockford-based parent Nelson Knitting Co. consolidated textile operations at the flagship Nelson plant, 909 South Main Street.

**ROCKFORD MITTEN & HOSIERY CO.,
400–18 SOUTH WYMAN STREET, 1911.**
Swedish immigrant John Nelson's 1870
invention of parallel-row knitting machinery
capable of producing a seamless cotton sock
revolutionized the nation's knitting industry
and gave rise to Rockford's textile industry.
Nelson and his sons parlayed the machine and
their revolutionary "Rockford Sock" into a
three-firm dynasty: Nelson Knitting Co.
(1870–1992); Forest City Knitting Co.
(1890–1954); and Rockford Mitten & Hosiery
Co., established in 1881 and later sold to
William Ziock and renamed Rockford Textile
Mills. Additionally, a number of competing
Rockford textile upstarts began operations. But
for all its initial vitality, Rockford's knitting
industry, which had supported over 3,000
workers and produced thousands of tons of
goods annually at its height, was virtually non-
existent by 1960. In 1955, Rockford Textile
Mills relocated to Tennessee in pursuit of
cheaper land, labor, and materials.

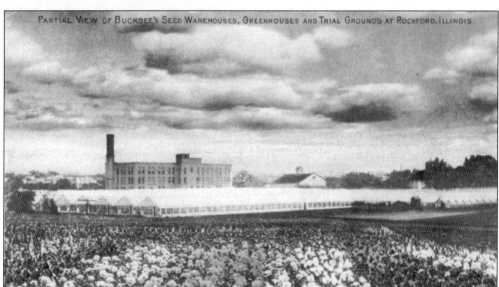

BUCKBEE WAREHOUSE, GREENHOUSES, AND TRIAL GROUNDS. Rockford gained worldwide
acclaim for its quality seeds thanks to four prominent mail order seed and plant wholesalers:
Roland H. Shumway (1870), Hiram W. Buckbee (1871), Alneer Brothers (1902), and Condon
Brothers (1910). Buckbee operations encompassed this 350,000-square-foot warehouse
(1899–1944), greenhouse complex, experimental trial area, and massive 15,000-acre seed farm on
the old Buckbee homestead near Kishwaukee and Broadway. The four Rockford rivals would
later merge, eventually forming seed giant Condon-Shumway. The firm lasted into the 1970s,
counting stars Bing Crosby and Perry Como among its loyal clients.

ROCKFORD WATCH CO., 319–25 SOUTH MADISON STREET, 1911. One of Rockford's best-known early consumer products was Rockford Watch Company's celebrated Rockford Watch. Lauded for their quality craftsmanship and precision timekeeping, Rockford watches were an integral component in running the nation's military and railroad industry. Rockford's largest employer in 1891, Rockford Watch was founded in 1873 by former cooper and future Rockford mayor Levi Rhoades (1830–91). At its height, the company's daily production reached 200 pocket watches spanning 20 grades. Despite its fine reputation, Rockford Watch ran down due to financial difficulties in 1915. Later home to the Rockford Board of Education, W.F. and John Barnes Co., and Ingersoll International, this complex today houses Abrasive Machining Inc. and Rockford Linear Actuation, Inc.

ROCKFORD WATCH CO. ADVERTISING POSTCARD, 1910. A prolific advertiser in numerous mediums, Rockford Watch Co. made a co-op splash nationally with a colorful, light-hearted series of 12 advertising postcards issued monthly between November 1909 and November 1910, including this Fourth of July–themed postcard issued in partnership with Flemington, New Jersey jeweler S.L. Hart. The postcard series, which promoted the company's famed "True Time for a Lifetime" Rockford Watch, included pre-printed co-op advertising messages on the reverse side.

FOREST CITY POULTRY YARDS. Because Rockford quickly developed into a major Illinois and U.S. manufacturing center, the city's close ties to Winnebago County's agricultural economy is often overlooked. This advertising postcard from R.E. Breckenridge's Forest City Poultry Yards offers a reminder of Rockford's agricultural roots. A breeder and shipper of "pure bred poultry," Forest City specialized in "eggs for hatching in season" and a variety of live poultry. Early 1900s competitors included W.C. Murtfeldt, Roe & Lundine, Auburndale, G.H. Chamberlain, and the Twin Elms Poultry Farm at Corey's Bluff on South Main.

EMERSON-BRANTINGHAM CO. ADVERTISING CARD, 1912. From 1852–1970, Rockford was a major manufacturer of agricultural implements thanks to John H. Manny & Co. and its successors: Emerson, Talcott & Co., Emerson-Brantingham Co., and Racine, Wisconsin-based J.I. Case Company's "Rockford Works." By World War I, Emerson-Brantingham's sprawling 1,700-employee manufacturing facility encompassed a 24-building, 175-acre complex at 500 South Independence Avenue that was regarded as the world's largest infrastructure for manufacturing agricultural machinery. Emerson-Brantingham struggled for a decade before its 1928 acquisition by Case, which closed its aging Rockford operations in 1970. Unable to find a buyer for its sprawling Rockford Works, Case donated the site and its 1.4 million–square-feet of buildings to the City of Rockford for use as the City Yards.

Four
RESIDENTIAL
ROCKFORD

FLORENCE MAY APARTMENTS, 207–11 NORTH WYMAN STREET. Downtown's Florence May Apartments once ranked among Rockford's most prestigious apartment buildings. Visible at center is the *c.* 1857 Rockford Gas Light and Coke Co. Building. Both structures were purchased and demolished by neighboring Central National Bank between 1959 and 1962 to provide expanded parking and drive-in banking facilities. The site is now occupied by a municipal parking lot.

COLONEL THOMAS G. LAWLER HOME, 218 KISHWAUKEE STREET, 1910. One of Rockford's most prominent Civil War veterans, Thomas G. Lawyer served with the 19th Illinois Infantry at Stone River, Chickamauga, Missionary Ridge, and Atlanta and was later named colonel of the Third Illinois Infantry. A four-term Rockford postmaster, Lawler was active as a local, state, and national commander of the Washington D.C.-based Grand Army of the Republic veteran's organization. The Lawler home was razed for commercial development in 1951.

"ANNETTE," 1907. Hoping to entice Buchanan, Michigan resident Miss Edna Rutledge to pay her a visit in Rockford, writer Annette noted, "You surely must come for I am waiting for you." Setting an enviable service record in horse-and-buggy and train days that the United States Post Office would be hard-pressed to match today with its automated sorting equipment and mechanized transport, this postcard was postmarked in Rockford at 6:30 p.m. on November 19th and was stamped "Rec'd" at 6:30 a.m. the following morning in Buchanan, 191 miles distant. Perhaps most amazing—all that service for a mere penny.

ZIOCK BLOCK, 1912. The block bounded by North Winnebago, North Court, West Jefferson, and Mulberry Streets was once home to these brick "Ziock Square" duplexes, built by Rockford Mitten and Hosiery Co. president William H. Ziock for occupancy by his textile workers. A 55-year downtown fixture before being leveled for urban renewal in 1958, Ziock Square was considered "one of the most amazing housing projects of Rockford's early history." Developed in 1903, Ziock Square encompassed 14 duplexes and one 4-family unit. Lavish by typical company housing standards, Ziock Square dwellings were large and well-appointed, boasting two parlors, a kitchen, a formal dining room, and four bedrooms.

F.G. SHOUDY RESIDENCE, 1003 NORTH SECOND STREET, 1911. This *c.* 1892 plantation-styled residence housed Fred G. Shoudy, founder of Rockford Wholesale Grocery Co., once one of the Midwest's largest grocery wholesalers. Shoudy lived here until his 1918 death. In 1933–34, the former Shoudy residence and several neighboring homes were razed to make way for the Jesse Barlogga-designed home of L. Harold Clark, son of 1904 Clarcor founder John L. Clark.

DR. WILLIAM H. FITCH & G.O. FORBES RESIDENCES, 849 AND 841 NORTH MAIN STREET, 1912. Neighborhoods immediately north of downtown Rockford along Main, Church, and Court Streets were prestigious addresses. Among North Main's notable residents were prominent physician Dr. William H. Fitch and foundry scion George O. Forbes. The Fitch home was razed in the early 1960s for the western approach of the $1.2 million Whitman Street Bridge, opened July 1962. The Forbes home still stands.

WALTER A. FORBES RESIDENCE, 633 NORTH MAIN STREET. Walter A. Forbes and brothers Harry F. and George O. Forbes were among the four generations that headed Rockford's Gunite Foundries Corp., founded by immigrant Scot Duncan Forbes and son Alexander D. Forbes in 1854. Home to grandson Walter Forbes until his 1940 death, the home was demolished in the mid–1950s for a new downtown Rockford Sears department store, today's Riverfront Museum Park. (Courtesy: Mark D. Fry.)

RALPH EMERSON SR. RESIDENCE, 427 NORTH CHURCH STREET. Famed Rockford agricultural implement manufacturer Ralph Emerson Sr. and his surviving family owned this once-familiar home between 1858 and 1932. Built in 1855 by Emerson's cousin, Second Congregational Church pastor Rev. Joseph Emerson, Ralph Emerson bought the home in 1858, expanding the once-modest residence to accommodate his family, which grew to include three sons and five daughters. Major additions by Emerson in 1865 and 1886, in addition to near-constant remodeling, eventually turned the structure into a 30-room mansion.

C.F. HENRY RESIDENCE, 112 GLEN ROAD. As the old real estate mantra goes, "Location. Location. Location." Commanding hillside riverfront views of the picturesque Rock River and Sinnissippi Park from the Rock's west bank have long made for prime, desirable, and premium-priced real estate in Rockford's near northwest side, North End. This palatial riverfront Churchill's Grove residence was home to leading downtown clothing retailer Christian F. Henry. The longtime owner of C.F. Henry Clothing Co., Henry also owned downtown's C.F. Henry Block.

BURR HEIGHTS, 1909. This impressive brick gatehouse along North Second Street served as the entryway into the wooded grounds and palatial mansion home of Charles D. Burr, president of Burr Brothers Wholesale Grocers and its retail arm, Burr Brothers Cash Grocers. Burr Brothers (1883–1936) operated a warehouse at 216–22 North Water Street and three downtown Rockford retail stores, in addition to outlets at Beloit and Rockton, and Kings, Illinois. (Courtesy: Mary Lou Yankaitis.)

TINKER SWISS COTTAGE, 411 KENT STREET, 1909. Built in 1865 by Robert Hall Tinker, a prominent Rockford businessman, politician, park district founder, and self-taught landscape architect, the 20-room chalet-styled Tinker Swiss Cottage today ranks as one of Rockford's premier tourist attractions. The National Register-listed home sits on a tree-shaded 5.81-acre site overlooking Kent Creek from a dramatic limestone bluff. Tinker Swiss Cottage opened as a Rockford Park District museum facility in 1943.

EAST STATE STREET, 1909. East State Street east of downtown was a prestigious Rockford neighborhood in the 1800s and early 1900s. Notable East State Street residents included immigrant Swedish industrialist and venture capitalist Pehr August "P.A." Peterson, immigrant German wholesale meatpacker Leonard Schmauss, and banker-turned-manufacturer Chester C. Briggs. One classic survivor of East State's former grandeur is the National Register-listed *c.* 1873 Lake-Peterson House, 1313 East State, considered one of Illinois's best surviving examples of Victorian Gothic residential architecture.

RESIDENCE VIEW, SOUTH THIRD STREET. This downtown residential neighborhood is today part of Rockford's National Register-listed Haight Village Historic District, one of the city's most fashionable residential areas in the 19th and early 20th centuries. Once home to Rockford's leading Spafford banking family and immigrant Swedish Erlander family, the gentrified 13-block Haight Village District includes early modest Gothic and Greek Revival homes, the delicate Italianates popular in the 1870s and 1880s and the flamboyant Queen Annes and Victorians popular in the 1890s. (Courtesy: Midway Village & Museum Center.)

59

NORTH MAIN STREET LOOKING NORTH. Rockford has been famed as the "Forest City" since the mid-1850s, when *New York Tribune* writer Bayard Taylor is said to have coined the time-honored moniker after visiting the city several times on the nation's lecture circuit. North Main Street, pictured here, was among the city's most prestigious addresses in the 1800s and early 1900s. Rockford's expanding downtown would eventually take over much of this area with a variety of commercial and park developments. (Courtesy: Mark D. Fry.)

NORTH CHURCH STREET FROM HASKELL PARK. From the 1850s into the late 1890s, many of Rockford's leading families built stately homes in this once-prestigious near northwest side neighborhood immediately north of downtown, an area roughly encompassing Park Avenue, Whitman Street, the Rock River, and North Court Streets, with the most prestigious addresses along North Main and North Church Streets. In its halcyon days in the 1800s and early 1900s, this neighborhood was home to some of the city's most prominent industrial, business, and civic leaders. (Courtesy: Midway Village & Museum Center.)

60

LOOKING WEST ON PARK AVENUE FROM NORTH MAIN. Running eight blocks from Wyman Street and riverfront Beattie Park to Kilburn Avenue and Fairgrounds Park, downtown's Park Avenue was once one of Rockford's more celebrated urban neighborhoods. The area comprising today's National Register-listed Beattie Park (out of view at far right) was the longtime home of Rockford's prominent Beattie family. Irish-born Scotsman John Beattie bought the 3.38-acre tract soon after his 1837 arrival. Beattie daughters Mary and Anna donated the family homestead to the Rockford Park District in 1921. (Courtesy: Mark D. Fry.)

Residence View of National Avenue, Rockford, Ill.

RESIDENCE VIEW, NATIONAL AVENUE, 1911. Today home to some of the most expensive and elegant old homes in Rockford, National Avenue and its neighboring "Churchill's Grove" environs once served as the 1862–63 Civil War site of the Union Army's Camp Fuller cantonment. Named for longtime early landowner Phineas P. Churchill (1804–89), the 29-acre Churchill's Grove subdivision was developed beginning in 1882. One of Rockford's leading residential developments, Churchill's Grove attracted prominent settlers including downtown clothier Christian F. Henry, insurer John H. Camlin, and Civil War veteran and multi-term Rockford mayor John H. Sherratt.

HARLEM BOULEVARD AND NORTH END BRIDGE. Since its 1882 platting for residential development, 29-acre Churchill's Grove has been an enduringly popular and famous Rockford neighborhood. Particularly prestigious Churchill's Grove addresses were—and still are—located along the subdivision's two major thoroughfares: broad, landscaped Harlem Boulevard and riverfront National Avenue. (Courtesy: Mary Lou Yankaitis.)

FROM SUMMIT OF COREY'S HILL, 1908. Much of the land comprising today's City of Rockford was once rural, as seen in this view looking north on South Main Street from the summit of Corey's Hill or Corey's Bluff, just north of Harrison Avenue. Namesake Alonzo Corey (1811–93) arrived in Rockford from New York in 1836 as one of the city's early pioneer settlers. Corey and his seven children farmed vast land holdings south of present-day Marchesano Drive on the city's southwest side. Heeding the adventurous call of America's frontier to go west, Corey's children eventually moved on, as did Corey himself, who died in Cheyenne, Wyoming.

Five

PLANES, TRAINS, AND AUTOMOBILES

ROCKTON-STATE HIGHLAND STREETCAR. Mass transit began with the 1881 debut of horse-drawn Rockford Street Railway Co. streetcars, which began to be phased out in favor of electric-powered streetcars in 1889. The fast spread of the automobile and the advent of public transit busses would eventually spell doom for Rockford City Traction Co. streetcars. In 1936, the last remaining vestiges of Rockford's drastically retrenched city streetcar service were discontinued, a day marked by the ceremonial burning of the streetcar Old 805 (1903–36) at Broadway and 10th Street. (Courtesy: Mathew J. Spinello.)

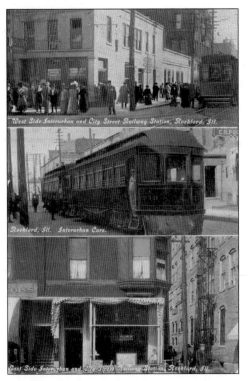

INTERURBAN CAR AND WEST & EAST SIDE INTERURBAN STATIONS, 1913. From hub city Rockford, the Rockford and Interurban Railway Co. (1900–30) operated inter-city interurban streetcar routes west to Freeport, north to Janesville, and east to Elgin, encompassing some 100 miles of track in four Illinois counties. The west side station (top), 126 West State, anchored downtown's busy Loop streetcar "Transfer Corner" at West State and Wyman, serviced daily by 900 streetcars. Downtown's east side station (bottom) was located in the Hutchins Block, 514 East State.

ILLINOIS CENTRAL DEPOT, 815 SOUTH MAIN STREET, 1910. Chicago's Illinois Central Railroad built this expansive $35,000 depot upon its 1888 Rockford arrival. The depot's landscaped grounds along Kent Creek were designed by Robert Tinker, whose landmark Swiss Cottage overlooked the site. The depot was razed in 1954, replaced by a new $250,000 depot. The colorfully named *Hawkeye, Land O' Corn, Iowan,* and *Sinnissippi* trains disappeared with the end of IC Rockford passenger service in May 1971. Passenger service briefly revived with Amtrak's *Blackhawk* between 1974–1981.

CHICAGO & NORTHWESTERN DEPOT, 505 SOUTH MAIN STREET, 1911. Built at a cost of $45,000 in 1893, the Chicago & Northwestern's downtown passenger depot served nine trains daily as late as the 1920s—three eastbound, three westbound, and three northbound to a Caledonia connection with C&NW's Minneapolis-bound trains out of Chicago. But with the growth of automobile and air travel, train travel declined and Rockford C&NW passenger service was cut back, and curtailed altogether in April 1950. The depot, subsequently rented for storage, was razed in 1963.

SHANHOUSE MOTOR SUIT, 1915. Beyond production of the short-lived Rockford, Cotta Steam Car, Federal, Rockoit, and Tarkington automobiles, one of Rockford's other early contributions to the nation's burgeoning automotive industry was textile manufacturer W. Shanhouse & Sons' celebrated Shanhouse Motor Suit. Given the crude state of early roadways and the frequency of automotive breakdowns, this was a common experience for early "autoists." Shanhouse's protective Motor Suit could be slipped on whenever the need arose to fix mechanical problems or change flat tires. (Courtesy: Mary Lou Yankaitis.)

CORNER OF STATE AND MAIN, LOOKING EAST. In the first decade of the 20th century, horses and streetcars still dominated Rockford's largely rudimentary roadways, days when nearly 100 of the city's 130 miles of streets remained unpaved. Major and prestigious arteries were among the first to be improved: macadam on Harlem Boulevard, cedar blocks and asphalt on Seventh Street, and paving bricks on Main and State Streets, as above. (Courtesy: Midway Village & Museum Center.)

STATE STREET WEST OF WYMAN STREET. The automobile made its Rockford debut in 1898, when manufacturer William Fletcher Barnes purchased an electric phaeton "auto-motor car." Initially dismissed as a passing fad, the car caught on quickly, as seen here in this West State view taken just a few years after the previous postcard. Rockford's automobile colony grew to 216 vehicles by 1908, a number said to have been one of the largest among comparably-sized U.S. cities. (Courtesy: Midway Village & Museum Center.)

NORTH SECOND STREET. North Second in Rockford and the old Beloit Road north of the city was once little more than a sleepy two-lane country road linking Rockford to Beloit, as seen in this view looking south toward Ethel Avenue in present-day Sinnissippi Park. Visible in the distance is the riverfront Skandia Furniture Co. factory. Although automobiles were becoming more common, travel between Rockford and points north was still largely by horse-and-wagon, Rockford & Interurban streetcars, or Chicago & Northwestern passenger trains. (Courtesy: Mark D. Fry.)

CORNER OF STATE AND CHARLES STREETS, 1910. Early roads were often designated by their far-flung destinations. Rockford's Charles Street (angling southeast at right) was once part of a much-larger state road named for its destination: Kane County's St. Charles. Once known as "the State Road to St. Charles," rural Charles Street grew along with the expanding city's east side, becoming a major thoroughfare with the construction of SwedishAmerican Hospital, Lincoln Middle School, and the Rockford Plaza and Colonial Village malls.

HAVENS LEAVING AVIATION FIELD, 1911. Famed pioneer U.S. aviator Beckwith Havens takes off from a makeshift riverfront Loves Park aviation field in his Curtiss Model D biplane during an August 1911 Rockford aviation exhibition organized by the Rockford & Interurban Railway Co. As part of Curtiss Aeroplane Company's newly formed Curtiss Exhibition Team, New York native Havens flew exhibitions in 13 states and Cuba between June and October 1911. Havens' 1911 Rockford appearance included a spectacular 17-minute round-trip Loves Park-Roscoe flight that left crowds spellbound. Havens returned to Rockford in 1912, making some of the nation's first recorded hydroaeroplane flights on the Rock River.

JIMMIE WARD IN HIS "SHOOTING STAR," READY FOR FLIGHT, 1911. Huge crowds gathered at Rockford's August 1911 aviation exhibition to watch Curtiss Exhibition Team aviator Jimmy Ward, seen here preparing for take-off in his Curtiss Model D biplane, *Shooting Star*. A Chicago taxi driver turned national aviation celebrity, "daring birdman" Ward's local exploits included a 12-mile, 10-minute round-trip flight from Loves Park to South Rockford Park, said to have been observed by nearly 20,000 spectators. Ward, feted in the *Rockford Republic* as "the first aviator to fly over Rockford…in a heavier-than-air machine," was said to have "proved the practicability of aviation" with his daring feat. (Courtesy: Mathew J. Spinello.)

Six

COLLEGE TOWN

MIDDLE HALL. Chartered by the Illinois legislature in 1847, Rockford Female Seminary (today's Rockford College) moved from rented quarters to its longtime Seminary Street campus just southeast of downtown in 1852. Colonial-styled Middle Hall, built in 1852, was Rockford College's first building. Dubbed the "Mount Holyoke of the West," Rockford College's most famous alumni is 1881 valedictorian and famed social reformer Jane Addams, recipient of the 1931 Nobel Peace Prize. (Courtesy: Mark D. Fry.)

VIEW FROM COLLEGE, 1906. Rockford College's hilltop campus just southeast of downtown offered this dramatic, sweeping view of the Rock River and Rockford's rising downtown skyline, as seen from the Middle Hall tower. The gently rolling oak- and elm-shaded campus, bounded by Seminary Street, College Avenue, Division Street, and the Milwaukee Road's riverside right-of-way, was purchased from Buell G. Wheeler in 1852 and served as the college's home until 1964.

COLLEGE CAMPUS AND ADAMS HALL, 1909. A strikingly beautiful college setting, the natural beauty of Rockford College's gently rolling hills, bubbling brook, and tree-shaded grounds harmoniously blends with the man-made architectural beauty of Romanesque-styled Adams Hall, opened in 1892. Rockford College's national reputation for educational excellence and women's rights activism in the late 1800s and early 1900s fueled enrollment growth. Rockford College encompassed 588 students by 1924.

J.L. ADAMS HALL, 1908. One of Rockford College's most distinctive buildings, $35,000 Romanesque-styled Adams Hall opened in 1892. Built largely through the generosity of Chicago resident Mr. J.L. Adams, the structure housed laboratories, an upper floor studio, and several "large, well-lighted recitation rooms." While the former Rockford College campus was razed and redeveloped following the college's 1964 relocation to its new 400-acre East State Street campus, the distinctive Adams Hall entry arch was salvaged, and erected on the new campus in 1976.

ROCKFORD COLLEGE SEMINARY, 1908. The heart of the Rockford College campus in the early 1900s was anchored (at left) by J.L. Adams Hall (1892). At center and right can be seen the college's three time-honored flagship structures—Chapel Hall (1866); pioneering Middle Hall (1852); and western wing Linden Hall (1854). In ensuing decades, the architectural character of the campus would evolve with the construction of several new buildings including a mid-1910s dormitory, the John Hall Sherratt Library in 1940, and the Jewett Lab in 1950.

ROCKFORD COLLEGE, 1909. The heart of the Rockford College campus, viewed from a different angle, shows (from left) Chapel Hall and Middle Hall. Writing to her mother in Milwaukee, daughter "M.A." provides a glimpse of Rockford College life shortly before Thanksgiving 1909: *"...Two weeks from tomorrow I will be home. I just can't wait until then, but I guess I will be busy enough. I will take tests in almost every subject before vacation..."*

BROWN'S BUSINESS COLLEGE, 101–07 WEST STATE STREET, 1909. Operating today as Rockford Business College, Brown's Business College was founded as Rockford Business College in 1862 by Messrs. Chamberlin and Dell. From 1892 to 1934, the college was associated with the Brown's System of Business Colleges, which operated 10 U.S. business schools. Renamed Brown's Rockford Business College in 1902, the college soon grew to encompass nearly 400 students and a prestigious ranking as one of Brown's top colleges.

Seven

THREE CHEERS
FOR ROCKFORD
HIGH SCHOOL

ROCKFORD HIGH SCHOOL, 200 SOUTH MADISON STREET, 1906. Nicknamed "Central," downtown's old Rockford High School was created in an 1884 consolidation of 150 pupils drawn from East Side High School (Second Avenue and South Fifth Street) and West Side High School (Park Avenue and North Court Street). Rockford High School, as seen here, was built in 1885–86. A sports powerhouse, RHS brought Rockford state boy's basketball championships in 1911, 1919, and 1939 and state football championships in 1902, 1903, 1905, 1910, and 1919.

ROCKFORD HIGH SCHOOL ADDITION. As Rockford grew explosively, so did Rockford High School, with additions constructed in 1900, 1906 (seen here), and 1914. Noteworthy RHS graduates included: pioneer aviator Col. Bert "Fish" Hassell; decorated World War II and Korean War Navy veteran Adm. George Dufek; 1980 independent presidential candidate John B. Anderson, Rockford's 1960–80 Republican U.S. Congressman; and E.J. (Zeke) Giorgi, Rockford's 1965–94 Democratic state representative. Rockford High's last graduating class, 1940, produced Emmy-winning Hollywood actress Barbara Hale, who played Della Street on the popular television series *Perry Mason* (1957–74).

NEW HIGH SCHOOL BUILDING, 1914. Rockford High School's last expansion occurred in 1914, with the construction of this Walnut Street addition. Vastly overcrowded with 3,600 students, aging Central graduated its last class in 1940, replaced by East High School and West High School. While the older sections of Rockford High School would be razed, the 1914 addition pictured here would become home to the administrative offices of Rockford Public Schools, Illinois's second largest district.

Left to Right, Kitteringham, Dowdakin, Keig, Ogilby, Ogilby, Chapman, Brown.

ROCKFORD'S STONEWALL LINE. Rockford High School's football team was once the toast of the town, as evidenced by this special commemorative postcard once owned by "Rab" standout George "Kitty" Kitteringham (left).

Rockford's feared Stonewall Line was anchored by a number of early RHS gridiron greats, including: left halfback and 1910 team captain Kitteringham; right tackle and 1909 team captain Clarence "Mooney" Dowdakin (second from left); left tackle Russell "Bus" Chapman (second from right); and fullback Irving "Crumby" Brown (far right).

A dominant Illinois football powerhouse, RHS lost only 16 games between 1902 and 1914, with only three losses coming between 1908 and 1911. And from 1915 to 1922, RHS amassed an enviable 58-9-5 record.

Even more impressive, the Rabs captured Illinois's state high school football title in 1902, 1903, 1905, 1910, and 1919, falling just short of the state championship in 1907 and 1908.

75

ROCKFORD HIGH SCHOOL BAND—TUBAS NOSTRAS FLAMUS, 1908. Under the visionary leadership of longtime school superintendent Peleg Remington "P.R." Walker, Rockford laid claim to one of the nation's most progressive school systems.

Supported with $300 in seed money from Walker, Rockford High School math and physiology instructor John T. Haight teamed with fellow RHS teacher Arthur C. Norris in June 1907 to create the nation's first public high school band, today a nationwide mainstay of high school education.

Charter members of the Rockford High School Band, pictured here outside RHS's main South Madison Street entrance, included the following: Ward Bacon, Lester Blewfield, Harold Bradley, Ritchie Dewey, Eugene Garey, Ellis Goldman, Hawley Goodrich, Bert Hocking, Ralph Hughes, Ivans Kern, Melvin Little, Hosmer Porter, Edwin Reber, Sigfred Sandeen, Frank Smith, Emmet Sullivan, Fred Warner, Clyde Weingartner, Robert Williamson, and Penn Worden. (Courtesy: Mark D. Fry.)

Eight

A LEGACY OF CARING

FIRST CONGREGATIONAL CHURCH, 607 WALNUT STREET. This enduring $60,000 Gothic-styled church, built in 1870 at downtown's South Third-Walnut-Kishwaukee triangle, far outlived First Congregational. Founded in 1837 as one of eight county Congregational congregations organized prior to the Civil War, First Congregational disbanded in 1914, shortly after this postcard was issued. Subsequently, Rockford's Masonic Cathedral was the longtime home of Masonic Lodge No. 102 A.F.&A.M., the former First Congregational is today home to First Assembly of God's Metro Christian Centre satellite worship and outreach facility. (Courtesy: Mark D. Fry.)

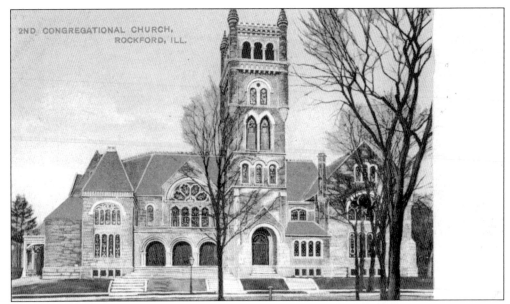

SECOND CONGREGATIONAL CHURCH, 318 NORTH CHURCH STREET. Organized in 1849 as a 41-member west side offshoot of Rockford's east side First Congregational Church, Second Congregational dedicated this church in 1892. While two disastrous fires struck the building in 1894 and again in 1979, the structure has endured its fiery trials. The congregation experienced explosive growth under the 35-year pastorate of Dr. John Gordon, growing from 200 to 3500 parishioners between 1912–47 and earning the prestigious distinction of being the nation's third largest Congregational church.

EMMANUEL EPISCOPAL CHURCH, 412 NORTH CHURCH STREET, 1907. Emmanuel Episcopal Church was founded in 1849 to minister to Rockford's transplanted New England Episcopalians and expatriate British Anglicans. In 1892, Emmanuel built this $36,226 English Gothic-styled sandstone church, (W.W.) Fairfield Memorial Parish House. In the late 1920s, plans were made to construct an adjacent $150,000 church, but the Great Depression halted plans. Emmanuel constructed its current $165,000 sanctuary adjacent to Fairfield Memorial Parish House in 1957.

(COURT STREET) M.E. CHURCH, 215 NORTH COURT STREET, 1910. Court Street Methodist-Episcopal was organized in 1852 as Rockford's second M.E. congregation. Designed by Rockford architect William R. Keyt, this $28,000 church was built in 1887. As the congregation grew, new facilities were added in 1917 and 1963. The distinctive church tower, destroyed by lightning, was redesigned in 1940. Ranking as one of the nation's largest Methodist congregations at 1,800 members in 1938, Court Street membership peaked at 3,000 in the late 1960s. Court Street Methodist, which survived a $1.5 million 1969 arson fire, underwent a $750,000 renovation in 1994.

WINNEBAGO STREET M.E. CHURCH, 1100 SOUTH WINNEBAGO STREET. Today's United Methodist Church of Christ the Carpenter, Winnebago Street Methodist-Episcopal began in 1852 as a southwest side outreach Sunday School program operated by Court Street M.E. Church. Organized as 30-member South Rockford M.E. Church in 1864 and later renamed Winnebago Street M.E., the congregation built this $22,900, 225-seat Modified Gothic church in 1903–04. The church was razed in 1967 in favor of the inner city mission's current $140,000, 150-seat church.

CENTENNIAL METHODIST-EPISCOPAL CHURCH, 219 SOUTH SECOND STREET, 1909. Rockford's First Methodist-Episcopal Church was founded in 1836 by five charter parishioners and circuit rider ministers William Royal and Samuel Pillsbury. An 1858 disagreement over pew rentals led 80 members to found Third Street M.E. Church. The two congregations merged in 1876, creating today's Centennial United Methodist Church. The congregation built this National Register-listed 900-seat church in 1882. An educational wing was added in 1955–56.

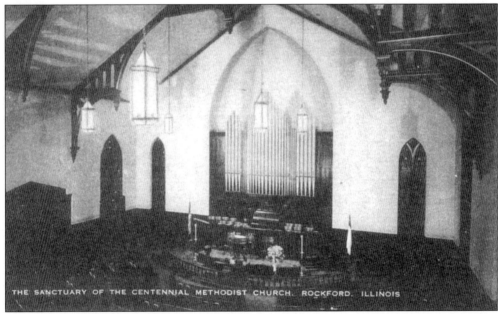

SANCTUARY, CENTENNIAL METHODIST CHURCH. While the exterior of Centennial's *c.* 1882 church remains relatively unchanged, the interior 900-seat sanctuary has undergone several renovations and remodelings since the time of this early 1900s postcard, as the congregation changed with the times and the denomination's evolving liturgy. Embracing its changing urban neighborhood, Centennial established its mission Iglesia Unide Metodista Hispana congregation in 1978. (Courtesy: Mark D. Fry.)

FIRST PRESBYTERIAN CHURCH, 406 NORTH MAIN STREET, 1910. Because Rockford's early Presbyterian settlers joined the city's already-established Congregational churches, the city wouldn't gain its first two Presbyterian congregations—First Presbyterian and Westminster Presbyterian—until 1854 and 1856, when many local Presbyterians began to feel they needed separate, distinctly Presbyterian congregations. First Presbyterian Church built this enduring church in 1905, constructing additions in 1924 and 1962.

WESTMINSTER PRESBYTERIAN CHURCH. Westminster Presbyterian Church was founded in 1856 by 22 Presbyterian members of First Congregational Church as Rockford's second Presbyterian congregation. Fledgling Westminster built this structure at South Second and Oak Streets in 1858. The 88-year-old church building was destroyed in a 1946 fire. By 1951, the congregation had constructed a new Normandy-styled church facility occupying an entire city block at 3000 Rural Street.

STATE STREET BAPTIST CHURCH, 602 EAST STATE STREET, 1910. Organized in 1858 as Second Baptist Church by 34 members of First Baptist Church (*c.* 1838), the fledgling congregation was renamed State Street Baptist in 1859. A longtime fixture at North Third and East State Streets, State Street Baptist built this $30,000 church in 1868. While the building survived an 1883 fire, it wasn't so lucky in 1949, when a blaze gutted the structure. The congregation rebuilt in 1951 at 1135 East State, home to New Direction Missionary Baptist Church since 1998. State Street Baptist, renamed Creekwood Baptist, today ministers at 7381 Spring Creek Road.

(FIRST) SWEDISH BAPTIST CHURCH, 530 EIGHTH STREET, 1910. Founded in 1880 by Reverend Ahlstrom and 12 immigrant Swedish Baptists, Scandinavian Baptist Church of Rockford, later First Swedish Baptist Church, erected this enduring Gothic-styled church at Eighth Street and Fifth Avenue in 1909. Renamed Temple Baptist Church in 1939 following the 1938 adoption of English language worship services, the congregation relocated to its enduring $400,000 facility at 3215 East State Street in 1959. The sender of this postcard was in town for a late summer tent revival at Swedish Baptist's "pretty little church." Subsequently home to Calvary Church of Christ and Emmanuel Temple, this central city church building is today home to Living Faith Tabernacle.

Swedish Free Church, 920 Fourth Avenue, 1909. Organized in 1884, Swedish Christian Free Church occupied this near southeast side church from 1892 to 1979. Numbering some 1,400 members by the late 1970s, the since-renamed First Evangelical Free Church purchased a 35-acre far east side site at 2223 North Mulford Road, where it built a $5.3 million, 2,200-seat church and an adjoining 2,800-seat outdoor amphitheater, Summerwood. The old church, pictured here, has since been razed.

Christian Science Church, 515 North Main Street, 1916. Organized in 1899, Rockford's First Church of Christ Scientist met in downtown's Mendelssohn Hall Building until 1910, when the congregation built this enduring Classical Greek-styled temple near Beattie Park. Offshoot congregations included the Second Christian Church at Freemont and Fulton (established in 1910) and the east side's Second Church of Christ Scientist (1919–39). First Church of Christ Scientist relocated to 4555 Spring Creek Road in 1977. This downtown church, later home to Christ Church Unity and Christ Tabernacle Baptist Church, is today home to Victorious Christian Worship Center.

Rev. Thomas Finn.
Rector St. James Pro. Cathedral.

St. James Pro Cathedral and Rectory.

Rt. Rev. P. J. Muldoon D. D.
Catholic Bishop of Rockford, Ill

ST. JAMES PRO CATHEDRAL AND RECTORY, 428 NORTH SECOND STREET. Organized as Rockford's first Roman Catholic congregation in 1850, St. James built this $20,000 church at North Second Street and Lafayette Avenue in 1866–67. An adjacent $8,000 rectory was added in 1873. St. James School, founded in 1886 under the direction of the Sisters of the Dominie, built an adjacent $17,000 school in 1891. The old school, since razed, was replaced in 1967–68. Following the establishment of the Catholic Diocese of Rockford, St. James served as the diocesan pro cathedral from 1908 to 1959.

INTERIOR, ST. JAMES PRO CATHEDRAL, 1914. With the creation of the Catholic Diocese of Rockford on September 23, 1908 and the selection of Peter J. Muldoon as its first diocesan bishop, St. James operated as pro cathedral until the 1959 dedication of the diocese's $1 million St. Peter Cathedral facility, 1243 North Church Street. St. James' sanctuary underwent a $100,000 remodeling in 1992 as part of the parish's celebration of the 125th anniversary of the building's 1867 dedication.

St. Mary's Catholic Church, 517 Elm Street. Built in 1886–87, downtown's St. Mary's Catholic Church was designed by Chicago architect James F. Egan in a diminished Gothic style. An adjoining parochial school operated from 1888 to 1974. Rockford's first Roman Catholic congregation built to serve west side Catholics, St. Mary's (*c.* 1885) since 1997 has operated as St. Mary's Oratory, a Latin Mass center and shrine operated by the Latin Mass Community under the direction of the Institute of Christ the King. St. Mary's subterranean grotto, patterned on a cave grotto in Lourdes, France, was dedicated in 1928 as a memorial to longtime downtown hotel operator Lena Chick.

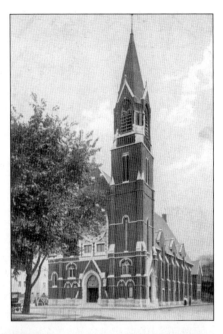

First Pastor

Rev. J. W. Davis

State Street United Evangelical Church, Rockford, Ill.

State Street United Evangelical Church, 1901 West State Street, 1910. State Street United Evangelical was founded in 1907 when the denomination's Illinois Conference turned its missionary sights on Rockford. With a number of United Evangelical families already living in West Rockford, founding pastor Rev. James W. Davis (1907–11) was appointed to oversee the fledgling 11-member congregation. First meeting in a tent at West State and Sunset Streets, the fast-growing congregation built this impressive $17,000 facility between 1907 and 1909. Numbering some 900 members by 1952, State Street United Evangelical Brethren added Education Wing additions in 1951 and 1963. Operating as St. John's United Methodist Church beginning in 1968, the declining congregation merged with Beth-Eden United Methodist, 3201 Huffman Boulevard, in 1989. Closed and subsequently sold, this enduring facility is today home to Mt. Sinai Full Gospel Baptist Church & Learning Academy.

FIRST EVANGELICAL LUTHERAN CHURCH, 225 SOUTH THIRD STREET, 1914. Originally organized by founding pastor Rev. Erland Carlsson in 1854 as the Scandinavian Evangelical Lutheran Church of Rockford, the ethnic Swedish congregation changed its name to First Evangelical Lutheran Church in 1927 to reflect its status as Rockford's pioneering Lutheran congregation. In 1882–83, the congregation built this $60,000 twin-steepled structure, the largest church built to date in the city. English-language services were added in later years for increasingly Americanized succeeding generations of Rockford's Swedish immigrant families.

TRINITY LUTHERAN CHURCH, 218 NORTH FIRST STREET, 1908. Organized in 1895 by 46 charter members, Trinity English Lutheran Church was Rockford's first predominantly English-speaking Lutheran congregation. In 1900, Trinity built this 800-seat North First Street church for $19,000. The congregation experienced explosive growth under longtime pastor Rev. Hugh M. Bannen (1896–1943), growing to 3,900 members by 1939. Needing a larger facility, Trinity erected a new 1,040-seat Georgian Colonial-styled church (1956) and adjoining three-story education wing (1960) at 200 and 218 North First Street.

SWEDISH EVANGELICAL LUTHERAN SALEM CHURCH, 1629 SOUTH SIXTH STREET. In Protestant circles, Lutherans enjoyed the largest church growth in Rockford between 1900 and World War II, organizing 10 new congregations. Among those was Swedish Evangelical Lutheran Salem Church, organized in 1907 to serve a largely Swedish residential enclave on Rockford's newly developing southeast side. Pictured here is the $175,000 Gothic-styled Salem Church, erected near South Park in 1910–12. Under longtime pastor Rev. J.A. Benander (1908–47), Salem's membership grew from 50 to 800. A $128,000 educational wing at 1629 Sixth Street was added in 1951. (Courtesy: Midway Village & Museum Center.)

ZION LUTHERAN CHURCH, 925 FIFTH AVENUE. Founded as Swedish Zion Lutheran Church in 1883 when a group of Pietists left First Lutheran Church, the fledgling congregation built this Gothic-styled church in 1884. Originally an ethnic Swedish congregation, English language services weren't added until 1922. As late as the 1970s, Zion was still holding twice-monthly Swedish-language services. Rockford's second largest Lutheran congregation at 1,720 members in 1938, a $200,000 mid-1950s renovation and expansion included a façade remodeling and a youth center/chapel/education unit addition. The church sanctuary includes a wood carving of the Last Supper, a Depression-era oak reredos and original stained glass.

EVANGELICAL LUTHERAN ST. PAUL CHURCH, 600 NORTH HORSMAN STREET. Already a hotbed of ethnic Swedish Lutheranism, an influx of immigrant German Lutherans into Rockford spurred the 1872 founding of German St. Paul Evangelical Lutheran Church of the Unaltered Augsburg Confession, the city's first Lutheran Church-Missouri Synod congregation. The congregation built this $16,342 Gothic-styled church in 1906, later adding an adjacent parochial school and parish hall. Severing a link with its ethnic past, German-language worship services ended at St. Paul's by the late 1940s. In 1996, struggling 80-member St. Matthew's (1967–96), 4881 Kilburn Avenue, merged with 1,000-member St. Paul's, creating a new two-campus St. Paul's congregation.

(FIRST) CHURCH OF THE BRETHREN, 1909. One of 14 new denominations to appear in Winnebago County between 1900 and World War II, the Church of the Brethren made its Rockford debut with the 1902 founding of First Church of the Brethren, though adherents of the faith had lived in the area since the 1830s. This South Rockford church at West and Morgan Streets was built by the congregation in 1907. Relocated to a new church at 2709 West State Street in 1923, Church of the Brethren moved to its current outlying 5.7-acre site at 6909 Auburn Road in 1963. (Courtesy: Mark D. Fry.)

CHAPEL, WEST SIDE CEMETERY.
Since 1891, this enduring
Romanesque-styled 100-seat chapel
has anchored Rockford's West Side
Cemetery, which was renamed
Greenwood in 1921. In 1852, the
Rockford Cemetery Association (*c.*
1844) began developing its West
Side Cemetery on a 33-acre North
End tract purchased from Charles
Reed, Dr. George Haskell, and
Nathaniel Wilder, adding an
adjacent 17 acres owned by D.C.
Littlefield in 1880. While this
structure still houses Greenwood's
crematory and offices, the chapel
has been idled as age and disrepair
have taken their toll. Today's 100-
acre Greenwood Cemetery ranks as
the largest Northern Illinois
cemetery outside Chicago.
(Courtesy: Mark D. Fry.)

JANE SNOW OLD PEOPLE'S HOME, 525–27 KENT STREET, 1914. Opened in 1908 as the
Jennie M. Snow Home for Aged Women, this "Old People's Home" operated until the Great
Depression. Reopened in 1934 as the Henry Puddicombe Convalescent Home, the retirement
home closed for good in 1935. The facility would later become the Children's Convalescent
Home orphanage, which relocated to Rockton in 1969 where it now operates as the Goldie B.
Floberg Center, a residential care center for mentally disabled children.

ROCKFORD (MEMORIAL) HOSPITAL, 507 CHESTNUT STREET. The Winnebago County Medical Society began efforts in 1883 to charter Rockford's first hospital with its newly formed Rockford Hospital Association, an initiative spearheaded by Rockford industrialist William Talcott and his sister, Adeline Talcott Emerson. A 15-bed Rockford Hospital opened in the Greek Revival-styled South Court Street home of Dr. William H. Fitch in October 1885. A since-disbanded College of Nursing was established in 1889 and hospital additions were built in 1888, 1890, 1903, and 1913.

ST. ANTHONY HOSPITAL, 1415 EAST STATE STREET, 1913. St. Anthony's was formed by local physicians to address the city's dire need for an east side hospital. A local fundraising drive raised $12,000 to purchase, furnish, and retrofit the hilltop mansion home of prominent immigrant German meatpacker Leonard Schmauss. Founded by five German-speaking nuns from Peoria's Sisters of the Third Order of St. Francis, 18-bed St. Anthony Hospital opened in August 1899. A major $40,000 addition built in 1902–03 grew the hospital into a 60-bed facility. Additions in 1909 and 1914 enlarged the hospital to 125 beds.

SwedishAmerican Hospital, 1400 Charles Street. SwedishAmerican had its beginnings in 1911 when ethnic Swedes began a $175,000 fund drive to build a hospital to serve Rockford's sizeable near southeast side Swedish enclave, a cause popularized through Rockford's Swedish-language *Svenska Posten* newspaper. Designed by prolific Rockford architects Peterson & Johnson, 55-bed SwedishAmerican Hospital opened in 1918. A since-closed College of Nursing was established in 1919.

Winnebago County Poor Farm, 4401 North Main Street. Today's River Bluff Nursing Home traces its inception to Winnebago County's 1853 establishment of its "Poor Farm" for the homeless, indigent, and insane on the 230-acre John DeGroodt farm. This Winnebago County Almshouse was built in 1883. Transformed into a county-run hospital and nursing home for the poor in 1884, additions were built in 1920 and 1930. During the 1940s and 1950s, operations largely focused on treating polio victims. Renamed River Bluff in 1956, the facility switched exclusively to nursing home care in 1957. The current $4.75 million River Bluff complex opened in 1971. Agricultural operations at Winnebago County's "Poor Farm" endured from 1853–1969. (Courtesy: Midway Village & Museum Center.)

WINNEBAGO COUNTY FARM SCHOOL FOR BOYS, 10104 FARM SCHOOL ROAD. The Winnebago County Farm School for Boys was founded in 1907 in Harrison Township as a school and residential rehabilitation services center for "maladjusted boys." In the Farm School's early decades, resident boys performed nearly all the chores necessary for farm operations. A portion of the crop went to feed resident boys, while the remainder was sold to cover the school's operating expenses. Herds of beef cattle and flocks of chickens were kept to provide fresh meat and eggs. The Winnebago County Farm School, later operated as the Durand Farm School for Boys, was sold to Rockford-based Rosecrance Health Network in 1973 and to Des Plaines-based Maryville Academy in 1989. The facility today operates as Maryville Farm Campus, a residential treatment facility offering therapeutic, education, and recreation services to youth ages 7–18.

MUNICIPAL SANITARIUM AND COTTAGES, 1601 PARKVIEW AVENUE. Rare in the U.S. today, tuberculosis (TB) was once a common scourge that claimed the lives of hundreds of millions worldwide. Known as consumption for the slow wasting death it exacted on its victims, TB was once a common killer in Rockford. Until a cure was found in 1950, the most effective solution for dealing with TB was sanitarium isolation. Built in 1916, the Rockford Municipal Tuberculosis Sanitarium (RMTS) was Illinois's first municipal sanitarium facility built under the Glackin Tuberculosis Act outside Chicago. Overlooking scenic Sinnissippi Park, the RMTS provided Rockford residents with free TB treatment. Cottages were added in 1917. The main RMTS building, as seen here, was expanded in 1927.

RANSOM'S SANITARIUM, 4500 NORTH SECOND STREET. Ransom's and its successors (1887–1964) trace their history to a failed 1869 Swedish-American business venture, the $10,000 Swedish-styled *Rosendahl* "bath cure resort." In 1887, the riverfront Rosendahl grounds and 20-room resort were transformed into Ransom's Sanitarium by surgeon and chief of staff Penn W. Ransom and his two brothers, physician Wilmot L. Ransom and counselor G.P. Ransom. Specializing in nervous and mental diseases and drug addictions, Ransom's served 19,000 clients annually at its height. Sold to Dr. Sidney D. Wilgus in 1914, Wilgus Sanitarium was later sold, and renamed Elmlawn Sanitarium in 1937. Closed in 1964, the sanitarium site was redeveloped for the North Second Street/Forest Hills Road "freeway" interchange and Illinois Park.

HODGE SANITARIUM AND REST CURE, 977–85 NORTH MAIN STREET. Founded in 1905 as the Hodge Institute of Magnetic Massage Cure, this private sanitarium was staffed by superintendent Dr. Edwin G. Hodge, "assisting" John L. Hodge, and osteopath Mrs. Minnie G. Hodge. Serving "nervous" patients, people "worn out from overwork, worry or disease," and those afflicted with such "chronic diseases" as rheumatism and stomach troubles, treatments at Hodge included massage osteopathy, electric vibrations, static and high frequency electricity, incandescent violet rays light, dry hot air, oil rubs, electro-vapor, and salt baths. Closed around 1912–13, this facility operated under new ownership as Rockford Sanatorium from 1916 to 1918. The site has since been redeveloped for professional offices. (Courtesy: Mark D. Fry.)

DR. BROUGHTON'S SANITARIUM, 2007 SOUTH MAIN STREET. In the late 1800s and early 1900s, Rockford was a sanitarium hotbed for those seeking cures from a variety of ills, stresses, and addictions. Between 1901 and 1918, Dr. Broughton's Sanitarium and its successor, Weirick's Sanitarium, were well-known, popular destinations for those seeking cures for alcohol and drug addictions. Located on a quiet, tree-shaded 12-acre site anchoring the Rock River's west bank, Dr. Russell Broughton's sanitarium gained a national reputation for its work.

PARLOR VIEW—DR. BROUGHTON'S SANITARIUM. The main facility of Dr. Broughton's Sanitarium (1901–16) was housed in the former $30,000 mansion of prominent Rockford architect and building contractor David Keyt. The sanitarium grew so much in its first decade that an annex was added to the mansion, doubling the facility's size. After founder Russell Broughton's death, the sanitarium was sold to Dr. George A. Weirick. The renamed Weirick's Sanitarium (1916–18) specialized in "Drug and Liquor Addictions and Nervous Cases." (Courtesy: Mark D. Fry.)

94

Nine
CAMP GRANT

"ROCKFORD, ILL.," WORLD WAR I SOLDIER AT DOWNTOWN RIVERFRONT. This unidentified World War I U.S. Army "doughboy" poses for a souvenir Real-Photo postcard next to the city's *c.* 1900 war memorial canon, located in the old Water Works Park riverfront esplanade at the foot of Mulberry Street, just southeast of Rockford's Carnegie Library. This soldier was most likely an out-of-town Camp Grant trainee, given the postcard's handwritten "Rockford, Ill." notation.

THE *MORNING STAR*—EXTRA! Following the nation's April 1917 entry into World War I, the federal government laid plans to build and operate 16 large U.S. Army training camps, including a facility earmarked for Illinois. A 12-member Rockford delegation met with Secretary of War Newton D. Baker in June 1917, securing the Army's $13 million Camp Grant facility for Rockford. Construction of Camp Grant provided an unprecedented economic windfall. Some 8,000 civilian workers were employed by Chicago-based contractor Bates & Rogers in the five-month construction of the 2,200-acre, 1,500-building military base. Once operational, Camp Grant pumped $1 million into the Rockford economy monthly.

ON THE ROAD TO CAMP GRANT. Sleepy rural country roads Kishwaukee Street and 11th Street were laid with cement and transformed into perennially busy thoroughfares with the construction and operation of the U.S. Army's sprawling Camp Grant training cantonment five miles south of downtown Rockford. Training some one million soldiers in 1917–18, another 250,000 decommissioned soldiers passed through Camp Grant following its post-war conversion into a demobilization center for 13 Midwestern states.

JUST ARRIVED—GOING TO CAMP GRANT, 1918. World War I U.S. Army inductees arrive at the Chicago, Burlington & Quincy Railroad (CB&Q) depot and train yards at Camp Grant. During both World War I and World War II, the country's railroads played a critical role in the nation's war efforts by moving trainees and troops, in addition to shipping the food and materials so vital to military success. In Illinois, the CB&Q kept a busy schedule serving Rockford's Camp Grant, which would grow to encompass some 4,000 acres by the end of World War I.

"GOING THROUGH THE MILL." Camp Grant's busy Quartermaster's Department was a mandatory stop for new U.S. Army inductees. Would-be "doughboys," still dressed in their civilian clothes, entered the Quartermaster Building at right. After "going through the mill" with the Quartermaster and his staff, inductees emerged from the building at left, clothed and equipped for their new life as soldiers in Uncle Sam's Army.

"Kitchens"—Camp Grant, Rockford, Ill.

"KITCHENS." Smiling mess workers pose outside their World War I-era "kitchens" at Camp Grant—kitchen tents on the left and outdoor wood-fired baking ovens on the right. Peaking at 1,689 officers and 48,854 enlisted men, feeding Camp Grant soldiers was a mind-boggling logistical undertaking requiring the dedicated efforts of a 1,000-man commissary staff. Daily consumption at Camp Grant included 225 quarters of beef, 800 pounds of chicken, 30,000 eggs, and several tons of bread, biscuits, and beans—just for starters.

"PLENTY OF BREAD HERE—AND ALSO OTHER WHOLESOME FOOD," 1918. With some one million soldiers passing through Camp Grant in 1917-18, the busy mess staff was an indispensable foundation of base life. Rockford residents, sacrificing for the boys in uniform, observed occasional "meatless days" and were daily subject to the federal rationing of meat, flour, and sugar to ensure "plenty of bread...and also other wholesome food."

BOYS OF MESS, 1917. The physical demands of army training at Camp Grant made for voracious appetites in Camp Grant's crowded mess hall. Training between meals at Camp Grant included any number of rigorous activities—battlefield exercises in the 12 miles of trenches simulating conditions on the European war front; target practice on Camp Grant's massive rifle range; training in horsemanship at the camp's expansive 500-animal Remount Station; and marching drills on the base's mile-long parade ground.

INTERIOR VIEW OF BARRACKS, 1918. Close living quarters in Camp Grant's several hundred woodframe barracks would prove deadly in September-October 1918 when a worldwide epidemic of Spanish flu hit Rockford and Camp Grant. In a few short weeks, over 423 Rockford and Winnebago County residents died from the Spanish flu, a shockingly high number that paled in comparison to the 1,400-man death toll at Camp Grant. Colonel Hagadorn, the camp's distraught commanding officer, committed suicide with his army issue pistol on October 7, 1918, in a "fit of depression."

Y.M.C.A. BUILDING, 1917. Far from home and hearth, the nearly one million World War I-era army soldiers that passed through Camp Grant were served by outreach services facilities operated by numerous organizations including the Young Men's Christian Association, the American Red Cross, the American Library Association, and the Knights of Columbus, a Roman Catholic men's fraternal and benevolent society.

SIGNAL PRACTICE. In the days before radios, field telephones, and satellite technology, keeping in touch with fellow soldiers and military units over long distances involved hand-signaling codes with brightly-colored red and yellow semaphore flags. Here, Camp Grant soldiers practice semaphore, an alphabetical signal system based upon waving a pair of hand-held flags in particular patterns. Using the semaphore system, these soldiers signal the dual-meaning pattern for the letter "J" and the word "alphabetic." Such communication duties were typically the province of specially trained Signal Corps soldiers.

AERO SQUAD, U.S. AVIATION SERVICE. Airplanes were a rare curiosity in Rockford until the U.S. Army established its Aero Squad training program at Camp Grant. Over the course of World War I, several Rockford "boys" would die in Aero Squad service: Lt. Clayton C. Ingersoll in April 1918 during aerial training in France and Lt. Fred E. Woodward in an airplane crash at Vero, Florida in October 1918. Ingersoll and Woodward were two of 73 Rockford men killed in World War I service. (Courtesy: Mark D. Fry.)

"OUR FIRST LESSON." Camp Grant rookies encounter their first lesson on the base's massive rifle range. It's unknown how many of the nearly one million soldiers who passed through Camp Grant in World War I were counted among the nation's 116,516 dead and 204,002 wounded war casualties. Camp Grant, deactivated in 1923 and subsequently leased to the Illinois National Guard, served as a Guard training center, and a Depression-era Civilian Conservation Corps camp. With the looming prospect of World War II, the U.S. Army reactivated Camp Grant in December 1940 as a recruit reception and medical training center. (Courtesy: Midway Village & Museum Center.)

"Strike One," Camp Grant, Rockford, Ill.

"STRIKE ONE." Baseball has been a part of off-duty military life since the Civil War, when Union soldiers returned home with a passion for the fledgling game. Impromptu baseball matches like these were literally the only game in town during World War I as volunteer sign-ups and a military draft of men 21–30 forced the mid-season 1917 disbanding of the Rockford Rox and the entire Illinois-Iowa-Indiana League. The Rox and Class B Three-I League remained idle until play resumed in 1919 following the end of the war.

"EVERYBODY HAPPY—LOTS OF FUN DANCING." Rookie World War I army soldiers and civilian Rockford women live it up to the happy strains of guitar and accordion music at Camp Grant. Local women often volunteered on base to boost the morale of soldiers through a variety of programs, organizations, and social events. Not surprisingly, a few wartime romances were kindled along the way between army "doughboys" and Rockford girls.

"READY TO CHARGE THE ENEMY," 1917. Coach Amos Alonzo Stagg's 1917 Camp Grant Warriors gridiron squad proved "ready to charge the enemy" during their tough schedule against area college teams and other military installations. Comprised of officers, largely college seniors with two or three years of military training, memorable Warrior standouts included University of Illinois end Ray M. Watson, Princeton quarterback Jack Eddy, University of Chicago captain Lawrence Whiting, and Fritz Shernik, a Cornell quarterback and celebrated "drop-kick artist."

COLONEL WARD WITH HEADQUARTERS 161ST ARTILLERY BRIGADE AND 333RD FIELD ARTILLERY REGIMENT IN THIRD LIBERTY LOAN PARADE, 1917. Fundraising drives like this Liberty Loan Parade spurred millions of citizens in Rockford and other communities nationwide to invest their money in government-issued Liberty Bonds to support the U.S. war effort in Europe. By June 1917, Rockford's several Liberty Bond Parades had raised over $1 million.

FOURTH OF JULY PARADE IN ROCKFORD OF CAMP GRANT TROOPS, 1918. During World War I, patriotic parades featuring soldiers from Rockford's Camp Grant U.S. Army training facility were a popular and common sight. In this aerial view looking west on East State Street from the Midway Theater tower, Camp Grant troops parade through downtown Rockford as thousands of city residents jam sidewalks and even, in a few cases, catch a bird's-eye view from rooftops. (Courtesy; Mark D. Fry.)

MARTIAL FAREWELL, 1ST ILLINOIS INFANTRY AND COMPANY A ILLINOIS ENGINEERS, SEPTEMBER 30, 1917. Rockford's Photo-Post Company produced this oversized 4-panel postcard, and scores more like it, to commemorate the martial farewells of Camp Grant soldiers as each company prepared to ship out from Rockford to their assignments at home and abroad. Here, soldiers comprising the 1st Illinois Infantry and Company A Illinois Engineers bid their ceremonial martial farewell. (Courtesy: Mary Lou Yankaitis.)

Ten

A River Runs Through It

ROCK RIVER SOUTH FROM MAIN STREET, 1909. This Rock River postcard scene taken in southwest Rockford provides a glimpse of the primeval 1834 view that may well have unfolded before eyes of Rockford's intrepid founders—expatriate New Englanders Germanicus Kent and Thatcher Blake and Kent's slave, Lewis Lemon. Settled as "Midway" and quickly renamed "Rockford" for a shallow, limestone ford just south of downtown, Rockford's riverfront location was prized as much for its aesthetics and fortuitous mid-point location between Chicago and Galena as it was for its water-powered economic potential.

Steamer Illinois at Illinois Park,
Rockford, Ill.

STEAMER *ILLINOIS* AT ILLINOIS PARK, 1910. One of Rockford's favorite warm-weather recreation attractions, the stern-wheeler steamer *Illinois* (1900–24) is shown here at long-forgotten Illinois Park, one of several unofficial "parks" located in scenic riverfront groves north of the city. Informal countryside parks like Glen Eyre Park, Illinois Park, and Love's Park provided bucolic havens for weary city residents seeking a few hours of escape from urban living, offering opportunities to indulge in the quiet solitude of nature and outdoor recreation with family and friends.

ILLINOIS **SUNK AT MULBERRY STREET DOCK, 7–19–08.** Using Eastman-Kodak's Real-Photo postcard developing paper, enterprising local photographers like LeVern Ryder sold now-rare Real-Photo postcards featuring breaking news events of short-term interest, typically local disasters. One of Rockford's famed Real-Photo disaster cards is Ryder's postcard showing the steamer *Illinois* sunk at its Mulberry Street dock. Rockford residents clamored for copies of Ryder's postcard, with some 2,000 sold within two days. Mere days later, the *Illinois* was raised, patched, and returned to service. (Courtesy: Midway Village & Museum Center.)

YACHTING ON ROCK RIVER, 1911. For local movers-and-shakers lucky enough to have a riverfront mansion, yachting on the Rock was as close as a short jaunt down to their shoreline boathouses. In the late 1800s and early 1900s, many yachting enthusiasts were members of the Rockford Steam Yacht Club. Two club members, John T. Bucher and former mayor Amasa Hutchins, operated two popular commercial Rock River excursion passenger vessels—the steam excursion yacht *Arrow* (1885–1900) and the famed stern-wheeler steamer *Illinois* (1900–24).

LABOR DAY—ROCKFORD BOAT CLUB RACE ON ROCK RIVER, 1907. Organized boating competition in Rockford had its start with the 1904 formation of the Rockford Boat Club, an endeavor spearheaded by a Who's Who of turn-of-the-century business leaders. Soon after its formation, the club erected a boathouse near the *Illinois* mooring at the foot of Mulberry Street. Pictured here is the club's popular downtown Labor Day Boat Race, one of many club activities and competitions.

CANOEING ON ROCK RIVER, 1911. In the early 1900s, canoeing on the Rock River quickly became a huge local craze, so much so that the Rockford Boat Club dropped power boating and crew in 1908 to devote itself entirely to canoeing. By 1917, canoeing had become so popular that over 400 canoes were in active use on the Rock by individual users and a variety of boating clubs including the Rockford Boat Club, AAC, Blackhawk, and Tea-Kun-Kha.

SKATING ON ROCK RIVER. Colder winters in the early 1900s froze the Rock River hard and deep, allowing Rockford residents to indulge in a variety of river-based winter recreational pursuits including ice fishing, hockey, and ice skating. More adventurous souls even attempted racing horses and cars. But ice-skating was, by far, the Rock's most popular wintertime recreational activity. To accommodate the throngs of ice skating enthusiasts, the city added wooden changing benches and electric lights. (Courtesy: Midway Village & Museum Center.)

KENT CREEK—VIEW AT ILLINOIS CENTRAL DEPOT AND PARK, 1909. This view along Kent Creek shows the breathtaking natural beauty of the high limestone cliffs inexorably eroded by the tiny Rock River tributary over the course of thousands of years. These beautiful southwest Rockford knolls attracted the attention of many early city residents, including the prominent Kent, Manny, Graham, and Trahern families. Native limestone was quarried in Rockford in the 1800s for a variety of uses.

SPRING BROOK NEAR NORTH END BRIDGE. The tiny Rock River tributary known as Spring Creek is still a familiar and picturesque sight just north of today's Auburn Street Bridge on the far northern end of Sinnissippi Park. From its eastern Winnebago County spring headwaters near the junction of Paulson and Orth Roads, tiny but persistent Spring Creek travels southwesterly to the Rock River.

AUTUMN ON KISHWAUKEE NEAR BLACK HAWK SPRING, 1910. While the Rock River looms large among Rockford waterways, there are several other picturesque waterways of note, including the Kishwaukee River, shown here near Black Hawk Springs in today's Blackhawk Springs Forest Preserve. The Rock tributary's Kishwaukee designation comes from the once-native Winnebago tribe, which called the river "Clear Waters." The Kishwaukee's north and south branch headwaters form near Marengo in McHenry County and just south of DeKalb in DeKalb County.

River View
opposite
Harlem Park,
Rockford, Ill.

RIVER VIEW OPPOSITE HARLEM PARK.
Given this picturesque riverfront view, it's little wonder that Love's Park was a popular weekend countryside get-away among Rockford residents. Located on the east bank of the Rock across from Rockford's popular Harlem Park amusement park, this rustic riverside Love's Park picnic and outdoor sports area would later be dubbed Harlem Park Annex for its spillover role entertaining Harlem Park patrons.

Eleven

THE LIFE AND TIMES OF HARLEM PARK

25 BIRDSEYE VIEW OF HARLEM PARK FROM SEARCH LIGHT TOWER, ROCKFORD, ILL.

BIRDS-EYE VIEW OF HARLEM PARK FROM SEARCH LIGHT TOWER. Hailed as one of the nation's finest amusement parks, 47-acre Harlem Park (1890–1928) was located two miles north of downtown Rockford along the Rock River's west bank north of Ellis Avenue. The $55,000 riverfront amusement park was developed by the Harlem Park Co., headed by Rockford Street Railway Co. owner R.N. Baylies and a group of local investors. In its heyday, Harlem Park attracted as many as 15,000 patrons daily. But by the 1920s, Harlem Park's popularity began to erode. In 1928, owner C.O. Breinig closed Harlem Park, moving some of its more popular attractions to his rival Central Park (1921–42). The Harlem Park site was sold to Beloit resident Benjamin Lyons and Rockford's T.M. Ellis for the development of their planned Rock Terrace subdivision. However, the two developers could not have foreseen the coming Great Depression and World War. The first Rock Terrace home wasn't constructed until 1948. (Courtesy: Mary Lou Yankaitis.)

HARLEM PARK PHOTO STUDIO. Photographic giant Eastman-Kodak's Real-Photo postcard technology proved a popular addition to the amusement offerings at Harlem Park, where patrons could pose for commemorative Real-Photo novelty postcards in the park's photo studio against a variety of backdrops, including the steamship *Rockford* and a Wild West "saloon" seen here. ("Saloon" Card Courtesy: Midway Village & Museum Center.)

RIVER VIEW OF HARLEM PARK, 1909. This postcard view shows how 47-acre Harlem Park would have appeared from the decks of the Rock River steamer *Illinois*. The *Illinois*, along with Rockford & Interurban Railway streetcars, provided transportation to and from Harlem Park, Rockford's premier outdoor entertainment attraction. Visible along the riverfront at right is the towering Circle Swing, one of the park's popular featured attractions.

BOAT LANDING. In addition to streetcars, another popular mode of transportation to Harlem Park was excursion steamboat. Two competing Rock River vessels hotly vied for Harlem Park business: the *May Lee* and the much-larger 1,000-passenger stern-wheeler steamer *Illinois*. During peak times, the *Illinois* made runs every half hour between the Harlem Park boat landing and its downtown Mulberry Street dock. Passengers traveling on the *Illinois* often danced on the upper deck to the popular tunes of the day.

HARLEM PARK ANNEX. While the southern section of Harlem Park was dedicated to a variety of amusements, the park's northern section was reserved for quieter pursuits including picnicking, strolling, people-watching, and quiet contemplation. Drawing crowds of 15,000 on its busiest days, many Harlem Park patrons took refuge across the Rock River at Harlem Park Annex, a popular east bank riverfront park better known as (Malcolm) Love's Park. An electric ferry shuttled patrons between Harlem Park Annex and Harlem Park.

ENTERING HARLEM PARK. Passing through the amusement park's main gate on Harlem Boulevard between Harper and Brown Avenues, this was the view that greeted Harlem Park patrons as they descended to the riverfront amusement park on the grand Main Staircase. Looking east toward the Rock River, Harlem Park's midway was lined with a variety of attractions including a lunch room, ice cream parlor, amusement rides, arcades, and the requisite midway games of chance and skill. Pictured in the foreground at left is Harlem Park's Laughing Gallery fun house.

MAIN STAIR CASE. Taking a reverse view from the previous picture, at left one sees Harlem Park's "Main Stair Case" from the vantage point of the park's wooded midway. Pictured at center is the popular Laughing Gallery. At right is one of Harlem Park's souvenir and novelty stands. Located near the busy main entrance in the high-traffic midway, this souvenir stand also offered patrons a coat check room and an expansive "Post Card Station" offering a variety of Harlem Park penny postcards.

HARLEM PARK FOUNTAIN. Beyond its various amusement attractions, Harlem Park was also a favorite with patrons for the aesthetic beauty of its landscaped grounds, which included decorative fountains, walkways, picnic areas, a riverfront "Lover's Lane," and plenty of towering shade trees. In a bid to heighten customer comfort and enjoyment, Harlem Park's operators installed numerous park benches and lights throughout the 47-acre facility. At left is the electric merry-go-round carrousel, followed by the Miniature Railway's Union Depot station.

AUDITORIUM, 1910. While Harlem Park's 5,000-seat auditorium hosted lectures, public meetings, vaudeville shows, and band concerts, the structure was most closely associated with its longstanding role hosting popular summertime Chautauquas sponsored by the Rockford Chautauqua Society, founded 1902. Traveling tent shows offering 15-day crash courses in cultural, educational, religious, and social improvement, Chautauquas were a national craze from the 1870s to the 1920s, when tens of thousands were staged nationwide. At its peak, Rockford's Chautauquas attracted over 80,000 attendees annually.

Dear Friend.   Rockford Ill aug 19 1905.
This is just like loop the loop only a figure
eight instead I tell you here is where the fun
comes in. All kinds of sport in the park.
We are having a fine time talk about your
fun we certainly are having it. Good bye.
                                                    Ellen

FIGURE EIGHT, 1905. In 1905, Harlem Park's owners invested $25,000 into a host of new amusement attractions including Shoot the Shoots, the Maze, an electric merry-go-round carrousel, and the immediately popular Figure Eight three-way scenic railway roller coaster. Harlem Park patron "Ellen" writes a glowing review of her August 1908 visit, *"...Here is where the fun comes in. All kinds of sport in the park. We are having a fine time. Talk about your fun, we are certainly having it."*

Figure Eight and Circle Swing,
Harlem Park, Rockford, Ill.

FIGURE EIGHT AND CIRCLE SWING, 1910. Among Harlem Park's most popular attractions were the towering Circle Swing (left) and the Figure Eight three-way scenic railway roller coaster, visible through the stand of trees at right. Popular large amusement attractions including the carrousel, flying Circle Swing, and Figure Eight were located near the Rock River to provide riders with a scenic view.

LOVER'S LANE. For generations, the Rock River has proven a picturesque and popular backdrop for romantic strolls. Where today's love-smitten couples stroll through Sinnissippi Park along the east bank's Rock River Recreation Path, turn-of-the-century romantics enjoyed a west bank riverfront stroll along this secluded, tree-shaded "Lovers Lane" on the north end of Harlem Park. Harlem Park's Lovers Lane disappeared along with the rest of the famed amusement park in 1928.

CARROUSEL BUILDING. Harlem Park's "Steam Merry Go Around" was replaced in 1905 by this electric Carrousel, part of a $25,000 upgrade designed to refresh the 15-year-old amusement park. Favorite Harlem Park amusements also included the Figure Eight, Shoot the Shoots, Maze, Miniature Railroad, Laughing Gallery, and signature "Famous Switchback Railway." Other park amenities included a dance pavilion, riverfront swimming bathing houses, penny arcade, novelty parlors, midway games, lunch room, ice cream parlor, zoological garden, steamboat wharf, and boating livery.

CIRCLE SWING, 1906. One of Harlem Park's oldest attractions, the riverfront Circle Swing or Swing Tower was also one of its most popular. Newer versions of Harlem Park's simple Circle Swing amusement ride, though overshadowed by flashier thrill rides, still hold forth at time-honored parks like Green Bay, Wisconsin's Bay Beach.

OLD MILL. Said to be a "great favorite with the romantics," the Old Mill operated as Harlem Park's "tunnel of love," a longtime amusement park staple. The ride, one of the park's newer attractions, was located near the Rock River to ensure the indoor boat ride with an ample supply of water.

Twelve

PARKS AND
RECREATION

Refectory Building, Sinnissippi
Park, Rockford, Ill.

REFECTORY AT SINNISSIPPI PARK, 1401 NORTH SECOND STREET, 1913. Soon after its March 1909 organization, the Rockford Park District set to the ambitious task of creating its first large scale park development, 123-acre Sinnissippi Park. Purchasing North Second Street tracts including the (H.L.) Rood Woods, the Cassidy Estate, and six lots from W.W. Sawyer's Arlington Heights Subdivision, the district began development of the riverfront park. The since-razed comfort house Refectory Building, pictured here, was built in 1912.

GATEWAY AND DRIVE, BLACKHAWK PARK, 101 15TH AVENUE. Having taken over operation of Rockford's small city-owned parks and spearheaded the 1909-10 creation of Sinnissippi Park on the city's northeast side riverfront, the fledgling Rockford Park District turned its attention toward the 1911 creation of riverfront Blackhawk Park on the city's southeast side. The 91-acre "Lathrop Woods" site, which sports a 3,175-foot waterfront, was acquired from William Lathrop and subsequently named Black Hawk Park in honor of the famed Sauk Indian chief.

EAST SIDE PARK, 400 EAST JEFFERSON STREET, 1910. Today known as Haight Park, 2.5-acre East Side Park, bounded by First and Second Streets, Lafayette Avenue, and Jefferson Street, was donated by Rockford's pioneering Haight family. The park site was originally slated to serve as the site for a new Winnebago County Courthouse to be built in 1876–77, but the new courthouse would be built on the existing west side Courthouse Square, 400 West State Street. East Side Park was later renamed Haight Park in honor of its donors.

FOUNTAIN HASKELL PARK, ROCKFORD, ILL.

HASKELL PARK, 400 NORTH CHURCH STREET, 1913. Originally known as West Side Park, today's 2.31-acre Haskell Park was donated to the city by 1838 Rockford settler Dr. George Haskell and his brother-in-law, John Edwards. The park was later renamed in honor of the prominent Haskell. Rockford's quintessential 19th-century renaissance man, the Dartmouth-educated physician, both learned and well-read, pursued a variety of diverse interests. Active in the community, Haskell was a founding Rockford College trustee and the first president of the Winnebago County Agricultural Society.

View of East Side, from Water Works Park, Rockford, Ill.

WATERWORKS PARK, 301 NORTH WYMAN STREET. Downtown's Waterworks Park (1900–53) was one of Rockford's most popular early parks. Created from land reclaimed from the Rock River, Waterworks Park provided attractive riverfront grounds linking the Carnegie Library at Mulberry Street to Rockford's municipal Water Works at Park Avenue. Civic and business leader Robert Tinker designed the park's scenic walks, gardens, fountains, and lawns. Pictured across the Rock River is the towering brewhouse of Rockford Brewing Company (1849–1940).

121

VOGT PARK, 1913. Located in the downtown triangle formed by Hall, North Fifth and Jefferson Streets, Vogt Park was typical of Rockford's early small neighborhood parks. Mrs. John Vogt and Mrs. A.E. Goodwin gave the Vogt Park site and a $1000 trust fund established for its upkeep to the City of Rockford in 1906 in memory of John Vogt. Tiny Vogt Park met its end in a 1958 extension of North Sixth Street for the North Second Street expressway project.

SUNKEN GARDENS, FAIRGROUNDS PARK, 1916. Site of the Winnebago County Fair from 1857–1902, the Winnebago County Agricultural Society's 22-acre fairgrounds enjoyed a storied past, hosting speeches by Presidents Ulysses S. Grant (1869–77) and William Howard Taft (1909–13) and serving as home field for Rockford's trailblazing major league National Association *Forest City's* (1871) and minor league Northwest League *White Stockings* (1879). With the demise of the Agricultural Society, the fairgrounds were sold to the City of Rockford in 1904 and developed into today's Fairgrounds Park.

LOVE'S PARK, 1908. An avid naturalist, longtime Fourth Ward city alderman and pump manufacturer Malcolm Love bought a rural 240-acre riverfront retirement outpost north of Rockford in 1898. A rolling, tree-shaded riverfront grove on the property dubbed "Love's Park" proved a favorite weekend outing spot for Rockford residents seeking lazy country summer afternoons full of life's simple pleasures—sandwich-and-beer picnics, hammock-swinging, badminton, and baseball, the popular national pastime. As Rockford rapidly grew northward, Love sold a large portion of the property in 1909 for a 95-tract subdivision marketed under the well-known Love's Park designation. In 1947, the area would become Rockford's first suburb with the incorporation of the 4,500-resident City of Loves Park.

DELLS OF ROCKFORD, 8786 MONTAGUE ROAD. Contrary to popular belief, Wisconsin doesn't have an exclusive lock on Midwestern Dells, as evidenced by the natural beauty of the Dells of Rockford. One of metro Rockford's most breathtaking but often-overlooked natural attributes, the Dells of Rockford exist today as Winnebago County's 369-acre Severson Dells Forest Preserve (c. 1976). Located six miles southwest of Rockford, the Dells derived their name from this secluded wooded glen, where picturesque 24-foot limestone bluffs rise along Hall Creek.

BURD-BELL BAND. Instrumental band concerts were popular from the turn-of-the-century into the Great Depression decade of the 1930s, years when Rockford supported Rockford High School's trailblazing high school band and a half-dozen company, ethnic, and community concert bands. Among Rockford's most popular community concert bands was director Charles M. Bell's 50-piece Bell's Community Band, which operated from the late 1910s into the 1930s under the Bell and Burd-Bell names. (Courtesy: Mathew J. Spinello.)

BEEFSTEAK CLUB, 1906. A Rockford outing club founded in 1888 by a group of young married men of means, the Beefsteak Club gathered for weekly summertime outings, traveling upriver to the bucolic countryside north of Rockford via the Rock River steamers *Queen* and *Illinois*. Members of the Beefsteak Club, feted as "some of the most influential men in the city," gathered at riverfront Love's Park for club meetings, cookouts, and baseball matches against rival outing clubs including 1900, Illinois, El Dorado, Entre Nous, and Soan-Ge-Ta-Ha.

CLAN MACALPINE KILTIE BAND. Today the nation's 15th oldest Scottish bagpipe band, Clan MacAlpine, Chapter 203 of the Order of Scottish Clans, was organized in 1912. Among those pictured are William P. Johnstone, Gavin Harvey, and John MacKechnie. Once known as the Rockford Kiltie Band, Clan MacAlpine is today associated with the Scottish Educational Society of Rockford. A favorite fixture at Rockford area events and gatherings for over 90 years, the Clan MacAlpine Bagpipe Band has long been associated with the Rockford Burns Club (*c.* 1858) and its annual observance of the birth of beloved Scottish bard Robert Burns. (Courtesy: Mathew J. Spinello.)

ROCKFORD COUNTRY CLUB, OXFORD AND WILLOUGHBY AVENUES, 1907. Founded in 1899 by a group of Rockford businessmen, the Rockford Country Club today ranks as one of the oldest country clubs in Illinois outside Chicago. Built on the 95-acre riverfront Eddy Farm, the Rockford Country Club's golf course and clubhouse were completed in 1900. The Rockford Country Club remained Winnebago County's only golf course until the Rockford Park District's enduring nine-hole public Sinnissippi Golf Course opened in 1912.

YMCA BUILDING, 104 NORTH MADISON STREET. Today's East Side Centre office building began its history with the Rockford YMCA, a longtime city presence from 1858 to 1862, 1876 to 1906 and 1941 to the present. In 1889, the Rockford YMCA built this $50,000 Richardsonian Romanesque-styled structure designed by Chicago architect Robert Rae. Sold by the faltering YMCA in 1906, the National Register-listed building has since seen use as the Merlein Block office building (1906–11), the East Side Inn hotel (1911–68) and East Side Centre (c. 1985).

YWCA BUILDING, 220 SOUTH MADISON STREET, 1917. Organized in 1891, Rockford's YWCA purchased the South Madison Street Frank Smith home in 1892 and soon added quarters in the nearby Thurston home. Additions to the Smith home in 1905 and 1918 provided dormitory and gymnasium facilities. The 1941 purchase of the Gregory House added additional dormitory accommodations. A new $750,000 YWCA facility opened on this site in 1958. In 2000, the YWCA relocated to a new $2.25 million facility at 4990 East State Street, adjacent to Rockford College. The former downtown YWCA is now home to the Salvation Army's Millennium Center.

Thirteen
ROOSEVELT IN ROCKFORD

MEMORIAL HALL DEDICATION, 211 NORTH MAIN STREET, 1903. Newly-erected $59,136 Memorial Hall is seen as it was patriotically decorated on June 3, 1903, for Republican president Theodore "Teddy" Roosevelt's famed visit to dedicate the Winnebago County veteran's memorial. The ceremony drew a crowd of 20,000. Observed Roosevelt of Memorial Hall, "No more fitting memorial could be erected to the men who fought such as this...a hall beautiful because of the uses to which it is consecrated." Roosevelt's visit also included a brief tour of the Glucose Sugar Refining Co. plant on Seminary Street and a patriotic parade through downtown Rockford, Seventh Street, and the Rockford College campus.

ROOSEVELT AT ROCKFORD, ILLINOIS, APRIL 6, 1912. Enthusiastic throngs gathered at Courthouse Square to hear popular former Republican president Theodore Roosevelt (1901–09) during a Rockford campaign speech at the Winnebago County Courthouse. Upset with the state of the country under his hand-picked Republican successor, Ohio's middle-of-the-road William Howard Taft (1909–13), Roosevelt returned to staunchly-Republican Rockford and Winnebago County to stump for an ill-fated third-term presidential bid with his independent Progressive Party "Bull Moose" ticket, a move that would split the Republican vote for Taft and send Democratic hopeful Woodrow Wilson to the White House as the first Democratic president in 20 years. (Courtesy: Mathew J. Spinello.)

ROOSEVELT AT CAMP GRANT, 1917. Unhappy with President Woodrow Wilson's longstanding pacifism policy and U.S. military unpreparedness as World War I ravaged Europe, popular two-term Republican President Theodore Roosevelt, a former Secretary of the Navy and famed Spanish-American War hero, returned to Rockford on September 26th, 1917, to deliver a 40-minute speech to 21,000 U.S. Army soldiers stationed at Camp Grant. Roosevelt's Rockford speech was part of a nationwide speaking tour organized by "The Colonel" to arouse public opinion in favor of active U.S. military intervention in the European conflict. Reviews of Roosevelt's Rockford speech, in the Democratic-leaning *Morning Star*, supportive of Wilson, and the Republican-leaning *Register-Republic*, supportive of Roosevelt, fell along expected party lines. (Courtesy: Mathew J. Spinello.)